Indivisible

Indivisible

AN ANTHOLOGY OF CONTEMPORARY
SOUTH ASIAN AMERICAN POETRY

*Edited by Neelanjana Banerjee, Summi Kaipa,
and Pireeni Sundaralingam*

The University of Arkansas Press
Fayetteville   2010

ISBN-10 (cloth): 1-55728-932-8
ISBN-10 (paper): 1-55728-931-X
ISBN-13 (cloth): 978-1-55728-932-2
ISBN-13 (paper): 978-1-55728-931-5

14   13   12   11   10   5   4   3   2   1

Text design by Ellen Beeler

♾ The paper used in this publication meets the minimum requirements of the
American National Standard for Permanence of Paper for Printed Library Materials
Z39.48-1984.

Library of Congress Cataloging-in-Publication Data

Indivisible : an anthology of contemporary South Asian American poetry / edited by
Neelanjana Banerjee, Summi Kaipa, and Pireeni Sundaralingam.
      p. cm.
   Includes indexes.
   ISBN 978-1-55728-932-2 (alk. paper) — ISBN 978-1-55728-931-5 (pbk. : alk.
   paper)
   1. American poetry—South Asian American authors. 2. American poetry—20th
   century. 3. American poetry—21st century. I. Banerjee, Neelanjana, 1978–
   II. Kaipa, Summi, 1975–   III. Sundaralingam, Pireeni, 1967–
   PS591.S68I53 2010
   811'.54080895—dc22

                                                            2010000744

To our parents, for giving us our first words.

Contents

VIJAY SESHADRI

BHANU KAPIL

VIKAS MENON

SUMMI KAIPA

MINAL HAJRATWALA

CHITRA BANERJEE DIVAKARUNI

SEJAL SHAH

NEELANJANA BANERJEE

Editors' Preface

Indivisible is the first anthology to showcase American poets whose ancestral roots lie in Bangladesh, India, Nepal, Pakistan, and Sri Lanka. The shape of the current book grew and metamorphosed over several years after we were approached by the literary publicist Kim McMillon. Kim originally suggested that we compile a short selection of local South Asian American poets, as a response to the fact that many of these voices had been diminished by the tide of anti-Muslim and xenophobic sentiment arising after the attacks of September 11, 2001.

As we started work, we quickly realized that we needed to broaden the scope of the book. At the time, there was no single volume that included a comprehensive range of South Asian American poets. While there were a few mixed-genre anthologies, these collections were over ten years old and could not possibly reflect the sociopolitical climate of the United States in the twenty-first century. Furthermore, many of those older anthologies grouped together works from both Canadian and U.S. writers. Yet the political fallout from the terrorist attacks of 2001 had made life on the two sides of the Canadian-U.S. border quite distinct, particularly for those of South Asian descent.

The fact that there was no coherent collection of such poets was all the more surprising given the contemporary boom in South Asian and South Asian American fiction. In recent years, such fiction has become extremely popular, with Salman Rushdie, Jhumpa Lahiri, Kiran Desai, Bharati Mukherjee, and Chitra Banerjee Divakaruni becoming best-selling authors. We felt it was crucial to complement this success by bringing attention to the many remarkable voices of South Asian American poetry.

Moreover, it was apparent that the number and strength of South Asian American poets had developed a critical momentum. It seemed a perfect time to gather together these writers and promote a dialogue among them. Consequently, we chose to focus on those poets who write and publish in English and who are actively engaged in the world of American literature. Regrettably, the limitations of the printed form mean that we were unable to include many of the fine writers working in the fields of multimedia and performance poetry, although we have included representative texts by artists such as Ravi Chandra, Sachin B. Patel, and Shailja Patel, whose work can cross from performance to text.

Indivisible brings together forty-nine poets, including long-established writers like Agha Shahid Ali, Vijay Seshadri, and Meena Alexander and dozens of younger award winners such as Ravi Shankar (the winner of the 2009 National Poetry Review Book Prize), Srikanth Reddy (the winner of an Asian American Literary Award from the Asian American Writers' Workshop), Maya Khosla (the winner of the Dorothy Brunsman Poetry Prize), Monica Ferrell (the winner of the Kathryn A. Morton Prize in Poetry), and Aimee Nezhukumatathil (the winner of a National Endowment for the Arts Fellowship in Poetry). In addition, we are delighted that our faith in our emerging writers has been shown to be well placed; during the time it has taken to bring this manuscript to publication, they have developed their writing, deepened their authorial voices, and built their publication histories.

Given the significant and growing body of work by South Asian American poets, we felt it was important to showcase these writers on an individual basis, in order to allow readers to gain a more complex appreciation of the aesthetics, concerns, and distinct contributions of each poet. In doing so, we also wished to move beyond the thematic layout favored by many recent ethnic anthologies, which often imposes academic categorizations on writers' work. Such themes seem all the more problematic given that poetry has multiple and shifting meanings and that poems lose something essential when they are divided up and pinned down according to thematic classifications.

In considering how to order the poets within the book, we were concerned that by listing poets chronologically (according to date of birth), or by grouping them according to their country of ancestry or region of current residence, we would only serve to divide the anthology—and our poets—into superficial groupings; much of the exciting resonances *between* poets would be lost. Instead, we chose to arrange the work of our contributors back-to-back, challenging ourselves to find new and surprising connections in their writing. As a result, established poets rub shoulders with emerging writers, and experimental structures follow traditional forms. For example, while Sudeep Sen's ekphrastic poem "Jacket on a Chair" examines the disconnection between cloth and body in Cezanne's famous painting, the next poem in the anthology—"The Mascot of Beavercreek High Breaks Her Silence," by Aimee Nezhukumatathil—presents the voice of the person hiding beneath the costume.

Working as editors, we were keen to ensure that the complexity of our poets' self-identifications (whether in terms of ethnicity, religion, gender, sexual

orientation, generation, geographical region, or any of several other affilia-
tions) was fairly represented and not used as a means to create divisions among
their work. As a result, we chose to ask each contributor to present his or her
own short personal statement. In publishing the chorus of answers generated
by this question, we hope that we are one step closer to illustrating the mul-
tidimensionality of our writers' identities.

Editing this anthology has taken many long months, but we have been
sustained throughout by our belief in the quality of our authors' writing and
the significance of this project. We have also been buoyed by a friendship that
has grown and deepened over these last few years despite our initial dissimi-
larities. In fact, we hope that these differences have added to the strengths of
our work. We come from disparate poetic traditions, yet working together has
allowed us the pleasure of broadening our understanding of a range of poetic
aesthetics. Moreover, while all three of us are poets, our other professional
roles have added to this mix: Neela as a journalist, fiction writer, and the edi-
tor of an Asian American magazine; Pireeni as a playwright, literary judge, and
scientist; and Summi as a literary curator, psychologist, and an editor of a
magazine of experimental Asian American literature. Our experiences of being
South Asian American—both the similarities and the differences embedded
in this term—also factored into our process. Neela and Summi were born to
Indian immigrants in the United States, while Pireeni, who was born and
raised in Sri Lanka and London, has recently made America her home. We
hope that all of these various incarnations have served to strengthen our work
as editors and writers.

The issue of whether unity and pluralism may be reconciled runs
throughout this anthology. We chose our title, *Indivisible*—a word taken from
the U.S. Pledge of Allegiance—in order to reflect some of the tensions that
exist between these core ideals. In this regard, we believe that this anthology
is a beginning and not an end. We hope that *Indivisible* will not only spark
conversations about the nature of South Asian American poetry, and prompt
readers to discover the interconnections among the poets gathered here, but
also encourage an exploration of whether America's infinitely divisible parts
may still add up to one indivisible whole.

Neela, Pireeni, and Summi

Thank Yous

We would like to express our gratitude to Kim McMillon for planting that first seed; to Sunyoung Lee, Jannie Dresser, Ravi Shankar, and Hayan Charara for their advice and fellowship; to Colm Ó Riain for his Web site wizardry; to Erik Dreher for his keen artistic eye and consummate skill in cutting up saris; and, most especially, to Khaled Mattawa for his verve, vision, and practicality. We owe all eight of you thanks for your generous gifts of time and friendship; Khaled, we owe you dinner.

We would also like to thank our contributors, for offering us so much help and encouragement and staying with us during this long journey, and our editorial assistants, Cristal Fiel and Beverly Quintana, who worked tirelessly on the final phases of this book. Our deep appreciation goes to Lawrence Malley and all the staff at the University of Arkansas Press for their belief in the importance of this project and for their unfailing good humor in these last intense few months.

Finally, we would like to thank our spouses, Colm, Erik, and Robin, for their unrelenting patience.

Introduction

Divisions

> A Mangalorean Catholic, I pray in Konkani, count in Kannada,
> swear in Tulu, sing in Hindi, write in English, and dream in
> American.
>
> —Ralph Nazareth

South Asian American poets have roots in a multiplicity of languages, cultures, and faiths. As a result, there will always be inherent contradictions in grouping together writers of such differing backgrounds. However, the experience of living and writing in the United States ensures that these poets share at least one thing in common: they are all active participants in the world of American literature. In compiling this anthology, we aim to encourage both an examination of what it means to be an American poet writing today and an enriched understanding of the South Asian American experience. In light of this two-pronged mission, we hope that this anthology might play a role in enlivening the ongoing debates regarding both literary and ethnic divisions within the United States and the nature of our indivisibility, both as a nation and as a community of writers.

While the history of literature is riddled with divisions, one key example of literary disunity is the split that occurred in the United States in the 1990s between writers claiming to represent quite distinct schools of poetry. Schisms appeared between New Formalism and Spoken Word, between introspective lyric forms, narrative identity-based poetry, and the theoretical constructs of Language Poetry.[1] Consequently, by the end of the twentieth century, American poetry seemed both overly academic and deeply divided, leading to a reduction in a general readership at home, while diminishing its standing abroad. In the last few years, however, the boundaries between these different aesthetic schools are increasingly becoming blurred. There is an exciting sense of the possibilities of cross-fertilization as a growing number of poets adapt and assimilate each other's techniques, themes, and forms. Nevertheless, it should be noted that this process of exchange and resynthesis is already well established among American poets with South Asian roots, many of whom have extensive experience of borrowing and transforming ideas from a multitude of different traditions. Such writers are often equally at ease with narrative form as with fragmentation, with discontinuity as with dactyls. Thus, Tanuja Mehrotra's "threaded ghazals" (a form Mehrotra created) merge the lyrical iterations of the traditional ghazal with the disjunctions of postmodern writing. Even when we consider the oeuvres of individual poets, we see a pluralism of form and content. For example, Faisal Mohyuddin's work includes both the long-form narrative poem, embracing history and politics, and short bittersweet satires charting modern-day love.

In his critical analysis of contemporary American poetry, Richard Silberg notes that the best U.S. poets today form "a distinctive sphere with many different parallel poetries, relatively equal, blurring and fusing across their boundaries."[2] We would like to suggest that the range of poetry being written by South Asian Americans today, with all its distinct and symbiotic forms, characterizes much of what is most valuable in current U.S. writing. We would argue that, rather than being relegated to a literary backwater, South Asian American poets are an essential—and indivisible—part of the landscape of American poetry.

As readers will discover, not only do individual poets play with a variety of different poetic structures, but our contributors, as a group, cover a wide range of styles and subject matter. In the course of editing this book, we encountered a popular misconception that American poets of South Asian descent were either engaged in writing about the sensuous pleasures of sequined saris or immersed in obscure spiritual tracts. The reality is refreshingly different. In fact, in many instances, the content of the poem remains unmarked by the poet's ethnic identity, as in Vijay Seshadri's "Elegy." The poets gathered here work with performance poetry and prose poems, not to mention sestinas and villanelles. They take us to symphony halls and jazz clubs, to supermarket aisles and basketball courts. They give voice to Renaissance women and Hurricane Katrina victims, Cuban refugees and German scientists. Even in those cases where the poets step into the ring to tackle spirituality or physical love, they adopt a surprising perspective, as we see in Subhashini Kaligotla's "Lepidoptera."

In this regard, it is interesting to note the difference between the range of poetry and the range of fiction in South Asian American literature. While the poems anthologized here reflect the pluralism of poetic form, voice, and subject matter typical of South Asian American poetry, this contrasts with the relative homogeneity of contemporary South Asian American prose. Both South Asian and South Asian American fiction are currently enjoying great popularity in the United States, yet such commercial success may come at a price: a closer look reveals that few of these best-sellers stray beyond the borders of magical realism and extended family narrative. In contrast, the American tendency to relegate poetry to a countercultural position releases it from the temptations of the marketplace. As a result, South Asian American poets have the freedom to diversify in unexpected directions, by either embracing different types of nontraditional poetic forms or tackling cultural stereotypes head on. The work of poets such as Minal Hajratwala and Ravi Chandra, for example, confronts the way in which cultural identity can be orientalized by mainstream markers, such as food imagery. In both "Generica/America" and "Cleanup on Aisle #3," the poets toy with the prevalent stereotypes of South Asian American food and culture, questioning the way in which such food metaphors can be used either to solidify ethnic categories or to subvert such divisions.

At the same time that literary critics and writers are beginning to trace a "free multiplicity of form"[3] in the poetic landscape, sociologists are pointing out that the dominant political discourse in America is moving away from fixed-role, binary identities (Us versus Them, foreigner versus native) to a more multifaceted identity.[4] We write at a time when U.S. national identity, like U.S. poetry, is attempting to embrace a greater sense of pluralism; for example, national census predictions indicate that non-Hispanic whites will constitute only 46.6 percent of the U.S. population by 2060.[5]

The question then arises as to whether contemporary U.S. writers reflect this changing perspective in their work. Writing in the mid-twentieth century, the literary critic Leslie Fiedler argued that Jewish writers were particularly representative of America, given that they grasped "that home itself is exile, that it is the nature of man to feel himself everywhere alienated."[6] In the same spirit, we would suggest that South Asian poets typify much of the zeitgeist of America in the twenty-first century. Through their writing, we come to appreciate how fluid identity can be, how it is an ever-active process of reinvention, a juggling act of many different histories and hopes.

The recent history of South Asia embodies significant divisions of identity, as the onslaught of empire and invasion was replaced by Partition and ethnic cleansing, the fault lines of religion and ethnicity dividing whole nations. This sense of divided identity becomes even more complex when we include the experience of diaspora. Not only does this entail the sense of being uprooted and of creating a home within a new land, but all too often it also includes renegotiating the boundaries of previous affiliations (whether as a Muslim, a Hindu, or even a brown Christian in a predominantly white Christian world). Moreover, the experiences of immigration and the color barrier are not the only divisions that South Asian Americans have had to face in recent years. The fallout from the attacks of September 11, 2001, have had long-term consequences for many Americans with South Asian roots, leaving them alienated and ostracized by the rising tide of xenophobia within the United States. Having formerly benefited from being considered members of a model minority, far too many South Asian Americans have seen their civil rights and citizenship questioned in recent years, as the nation's consciousness has proliferated with stereotypes of brown-skinned dissidents, sporting Muslim names or wearing threatening turbans. It is as if South Asian Americans went from being gurus to being terrorists in one fell swoop. We should note that during the course of editing this book, some of our own contributors have fallen prey to such racial profiling: in one case, a professor seen hauling suspiciously large bundles of paper (poetry manuscripts) across campus was detained by the bomb squad and the state police,[7] while in late 2009, a professor leaving a poetry reading in Manhattan was arrested and detained for thirty hours without legal rights for an unpaid speeding ticket.[8]

On the positive side, however, life in the United States, where minority groups are so often thrown together in close proximity, creates curious new unions and juxtapositions. While traditional political and ethnic tensions may still lead to divisions even in the New World (Muslim versus Hindu, Bangladeshi versus Pakistani, Sri Lankan Tamil versus Sri Lankan Sinhalese), at the same time it should be noted that the common experiences of diaspora and immigration may help to shape new alliances. Thus, the inclusive term "Desi" is used by South Asian Americans to identify themselves, embracing all those in the diaspora, irrespective of religion or region. This sense of changing identity—of transcending traditional divisions—is also manifest in the way that South Asian American poets create transethnic allegiances in their work. Their writing refuses to be contained within culturally prescribed boundaries. In Monica Ferrell's "In the Binary Alleys of the Lion's Virus," the poet conflates the experience of an American tourist with that of crusading Christian knights and of British Romantic poets taking the Grand Tour through Italy. In "The Blacktop Gospels," Sachin B. Patel portrays the way in which new pacts and loyalties form between ethnic minorities on the basketball courts of America.

As we consider South Asian identity within the United States, we see an ever-changing pattern of congruence and contradiction. This sense of new truths emerging from conflicting visions becomes apparent within the poems gathered here. Thus, while the Old World incubates within the New in Vandana Khanna's "Blackwater Fever," Agha Shahid Ali suggests a rupturing of the two worlds in "A Pastoral," asking, "Is history deaf there, across the oceans?" Similarly, while Chitra Banerjee Divakaruni's poem "Indian Movie, New Jersey" notes the importance of films as vehicles for the frustrated dreams of immigrants, Vikas Menon pieces together bad movie subtitles in his found poem "Urdu Funk," underlining how such films become symbols for our own confused identities and the difficulties of translation.

Articulations

As John Hollander notes, every true poet (irrespective of background) lives "a kind of diaspora in his own language."[9] The process of questioning the nature of language, of living at a conscious and peculiar angle to words, is surely heightened among writers who speak more than just one language. (Several of this anthology's poets either speak multiple languages or at least grew up surrounded by the sounds of different tongues.) In grappling with the inherent problem of translation—that is, that no two languages truly map precisely onto one other—we develop an enhanced appreciation of the fault lines of language. For instance, Agha Shahid Ali's poem "Ghazal" is an intricate meditation on language's approximations and translations. It begins:

> The only language of loss left in the world is Arabic—
> These words were said to me in a language not Arabic.

Choosing to write in English, the poet brings a fresh interpretation to the meter used in this traditional verse form and extends its typical subject matter, that of pining for a loved one, to encompass the poet's longing for his missing heritage. The poem's last lines suggest that neither language nor identity is stable:

They ask me to tell them what *Shahid* means—
Listen: It means "The Belovéd" in Persian, "witness" in Arabic.

From the cracks between languages, new ideas emerge. As poets explore such liminal territory, they call attention to the semantic dropouts between languages, heightening our awareness of how we try and fail to capture our perceptions in words. The poets gathered here propose novel ways of looking at the world. The writing of Aryanil Mukherjee, for example, examines the gaps between American English and Bengali. His poem "memory writings :: picnic" gathers its sense of primal menace from the Bengali word "banbhojan," which literally means "forest feast." As the poem unfolds, the reader begins to realize that it is the trees, rather than the humans, that are doing the feasting. The complications of being at once American and Bengali are captured by the imperfect translations and miscommunications of language. In "treeforms :: the touch of language," Mukherjee further embraces the messiness of communication by resisting the idea of "linearity":

well, I've always avoided this naiveté
the face value of linearity.
broken down the ant-lines on the wall
from here to childhood

For the author, the clean arc of narrative linearity eliminates the detours that make up our stories, erasing the richness of those experiences that do not fit a simple storyline. By weaving a manifesto into his poem, Mukherjee draws attention to himself as a biased narrator, asking for his own story to be interrogated. The reader is invited to engage in Mukherjee's critique of linearity and to imagine the missing tangents of experience.

Aryanil Mukherjee is one of several poets in *Indivisible* who draw inspiration from postmodern and experimental philosophies of language. As the presence of South Asians both in the United States and in its literature has grown, the diversity of aesthetics among South Asian American poets has correspondingly multiplied. While several of the writers in this anthology draw on lyrical or formal traditions, still others have been influenced by the works of the Black Mountain, New York School, and Language poets. In these American avant-garde traditions of the past half century, personal narrative expression—particularly the idea of an author's voice as unified, legitimate, and trustworthy—is closely examined. We are confronted with the fact that experiencing, remembering, and writing contain a world of simultaneous truths and untruths. Consequently, some of the experimental writers in *Indivisible* use nontraditional and nonnarrative forms to tackle the inherent pitfalls of autobiographical expression. Embodying multiple narrative voices throughout its structure, Bhanu Kapil's *Humanimal* merges personal and post-colonial history: the author juxtaposes the story of two feral children found in India in 1921 with her own experience of following a film crew to a jungle in Bengal, as well as with the texts of the missionary who found the children. In this way, Kapil's writing deliberately ruptures the boundaries of genre and explores the intersections of autobiography, history, and fictional dramatization.

A further way in which South Asian American poets engage with the "intolerable wrestle with words and meanings," as T. S. Eliot puts it, rests in their heightened appreciation of language as a political tool. In an era when Americans are bombarded with political double-speak and the half truths of the advertising industry, of "surgical strikes" instead of missile attacks and "waterboarding" rather than torture, there is a growing sense among U.S. writers that, as Wallace Stevens said,

> speech is not dirty silence
> clarified. It is silence made still dirtier.

Coming from the political turmoil of South Asia, several of the poets gathered here have firsthand experience of how dangerous language can be. In his poem "Lost Column," Ro Gunetilleke reflects on the ultimate price paid by writers who challenged the status quo. Describing the murder of the Sri Lankan playwright and journalist Richard de Souza, he writes:

> In the belly of the jungle,
> on a pyre of tires,
> they erased you
> word by word.

Other poems in *Indivisible* spotlight the way in which language is used to fabricate political fictions. In "nationalism redactor," Mytili Jagannathan

creates friction between concepts by setting up challenging word juxtaposi-
tions, deleting punctuation, and leaving semantic gaps within her lines:

> the sign dissolves the
> camera solves resisting
> bodies India day parade.

Such deliberate omissions force readers to reconsider the linguistic fabric of
Indian nationalist rhetoric and to reexamine its missing elements. All too
often, the disparate and conflicting components of a country's existence—
"women / lining up for water" against the backdrop of "Monsanto green"—are
left out of "redacted" or edited versions of mainstream nationalist writing. As
Jagannathan points out, events such as the India Day parade portray a false
façade of unity, while the camera can be used to edit out, or "solve," the prob-
lem of "resisting bodies" that do not agree with the dominant political fiction.

Similarly, in "Against Nostalgia," Amitava Kumar urges the reader to
question the narratives of an idyllic past. He writes:

> When you died in the house you were born in.
> When you knew who was a Hindu and who a Muslim
> and it did not matter.
> They were never there. Those days.

Kumar encourages us to confront the obfuscations of rhetoric and reminds us
of the power of open debate in shaping a more effective political future.
Addressing similar problems in the United States, Reetika Vazirani uses both
formal and experimental techniques to question our sociopolitical fictions. In
"It's Me, I'm Not Home," Vazirani employs the formal villanelle form to
underline the fragmentation of lives in the digital age, while in "It's a Young
Country," the poet uses disjunctures, midsentence drops, and phrases
snatched from pop culture ("*Can't hurry* go the Supremes") to create a sense
of the speed of American life and illustrate her ambivalence toward the
American dream. Vazirani writes:

> in order to form a more perfect
> some step forward some step back

By omitting the word "union" and effectively fracturing this phrase from the U.S. Constitution, the poet leaves us wondering about the nature of the "more perfect" entity that we might be forming.

Allegiances

> Great literature is simply language charged with meaning to the utmost possible degree.
>
> —Ezra Pound, 1931

American poetry has a long tradition of looking to South Asia for inspiration, going back to Emerson's close study of the *Bhagavad Gita*.[10] While many South Asian American poets writing today exhibit a rich American lineage—encompassing the pop-culture predilections of the New York School, the post-modern disjunctions of Language Poetry, and the introversions of the Confessional poets—some of these schools were themselves outgrowths of the American fascination with South Asian culture. The poets of the Deep Image movement, including such writers as Robert Bly, Louis Simpson, and Donald Hall, were profoundly influenced by South Asian meditational poetry. (In fact, Bly played a role in the defense of the Bengali Hungry Generation poets, placed on trial for anti-establishmentarianism in Kolkata during the 1960s.) Furthermore, three of the founders of Beat Poetry (Allen Ginsberg, Gary Snyder, and Peter Orlovsky) spent several seminal years studying and traveling in India, a journey that is reflected in much of their subsequent writing. Even Ginsberg's "Howl"—the quintessential American poem of the twentieth century—shows the influence of South Asian philosophy.

This tradition of poetic interconnection is perpetuated by the contemporary voices featured in *Indivisible*. There is a playful juggling of images between cultures as poets construct their poems. In "Draupadi's Dharma," Pramila Venkateswaran links the tone of Draupadi's protest to the confessional angst in Sylvia Plath's poem "Daddy," while Subhashini Kaligotla's "My Heart Belongs to Daddy" juxtaposes the vocabulary of American jazz speak with the ancient story of Ravana's kidnapping of Sita.

South Asian American poets transfuse a wealth of new images into the bloodstream of U.S. poetry. In Pound's terms, they "charge language" with additional meanings. Philosophical ideas expand and flourish in this fertile meeting ground, as we see in Srikanth Reddy's "Scarecrow Eclogue," where the question of literary responsibility is set against the context of Krishna's teachings on duty in the *Bhagavad Gita*. Moreover, the challenges of our modern age are framed by a deeper, richer field of vision. Thus, the immediate traumas of contemporary nuclear devastation and industrial disaster are mapped against the lessons of ancient mythology in poems such as Maya Khosla's "Oppenheimer quotes *The Bhagavad Gita*" and Vivek Jain's "Anand's Story," which deals with the Bhopal tragedy. The scale of current sociopolitical problems, such as colonialism, American expansionism, and immigration, is changed as these concepts are viewed through the long lens of South Asian history. Thus, the travails of landing in a new land are considered through the musings of a sixteenth-century Mughal emperor in Jeet Thayil's "Letter from a Mughal Emperor, 2006," while R. Parthasarathy forces us to reconsider the current shape of American trade imperialism within the context of the English and Dutch merchant-led occupations of Southern India four hundred years ago, noting:

Across the seas a new knowledge,

sudden and unobtrusive as first snow
transforming the landscape,
rinses speech, affirms the brown skin

and the heart beating to a different rhythm.

—extract from *Exile*

Yet the poems contained in this anthology do not just expand our sense of time. They also prompt us to reevaluate the dominant ethno-geographical divisions of the world. They encourage us to reconsider the boundaries that we take for granted. For example, they point out new connections between different groups as unrelated political rebellions are replaced by vibrant transethnic allegiances. In Sasha Kamini Parmasad's "The Old Man," a disenfranchised South Asian farmworker in the Caribbean empathizes with the Sri Lankan guerilla insurrection, half a world away; Meena Alexander, pausing at the brink of the Hudson after the 2001 attacks on New York, links hands, poetically, with her Japanese counterpart, recalling the American attacks on

Hiroshima. In this context, our poems resonate with the arguments recently put forward by academics such as Rajini Srikanth, in *The World Next Door: South Asian American Literature and the Idea of America* (Temple University Press, 2004), and Vijay Prashad, in *Everybody Was Kung Fu Fighting: Afro-Asian Connections and the Myth of Cultural Purity* (Beacon Press, 2002). Moreover, the poems in *Indivisible* demonstrate the transnationality that is increasingly part of the jet age of modern America: Shailja Patel's "Shilling Love" traces her life journey from Kenya to Britain to the United States, while Reena Narayan's "Tobacco Wrapped in *The Fiji Times*" shows the American poet discovering her roots in the Pacific islands. This sense of multiple migrations is reflected in the poets themselves, some of whom currently keep homes in several countries.

Here are poems portraying allegiances and paradoxes that reverberate all the more deeply because they encourage the reader to pause and reconsider the semantics of our present world. In Ralph Nazareth's "Horse Play," a father attempting to demonstrate to his small son how the glories of India withstood Alexander the Great ironically finds his American child harboring his own agenda of possession. One single culture appears to triumph, and yet, in "Made in India, Immigrant Song #3," Purvi Shah shows us how South Asia has insinuated itself into the very fabric of Manhattan's sidewalks. The poems in *Indivisible* repeatedly demonstrate that there is no single, simple political truth. Instead, they complicate meanings, present new perspectives, and make us question the very ground on which we stand.

Notes

1. *20th Century American Poetics: Poets on the Art of Poetry,* ed. D. Gioia, D. Mason, and M. Shoerke (New York: McGraw Hill, 2003).

2. Richard Silberg, *Reading the Sphere: A Geography of Contemporary American Poetry.* (Berkeley: Berkeley Hill Books, 2001), 40.

3. Mark Wallace, "Toward a Free Multiplicity of Form," in *Telling It Slant: Avant-Garde Poetics of the 1990s,* ed. M. Wallace and S. Marks (Tuscaloosa: University of Alabama Press, 2003), 196.

4. Stuart Hall, " The Question of Cultural Identity," in *Readings in Contemporary Political Sociology,* ed. K. Nash (Malden, MA: Blackwell, 2000).

5. Frank Pellegrini, "The Coming of the Minority Majority," *Time Magazine.* August 31, 2000.

6. Leslie Fiedler, *Waiting for the End* (New York: Stein & Day, 1964).

7. Kazim Ali, "Culture of Fear: Professor of Poetry Becomes Terror Suspect," *New America Media,* April 21, 2007.

8. Ravi Shankar, "Wrongly Jailed in NYC: Making a Joke Out of Justice," *Hartford Courant,* August 2, 2009.

9. John Hollander, "The Question of Jewish American Poetry," in *What Is Jewish Literature,* ed. Hana Wirth-Nesher (Philadelphia: Jewish Publication Society, 1994).

10. Richard Geldard, *The Spiritual Teachings of Ralph Waldo Emerson,* 2nd ed. (Herndon, VA: Lindisfarne Books, 2001), 55.

Indivisible

REETIKA VAZIRANI

Reetika Vazirani was born in India in 1962 and moved to the United States in 1967. She received her BA from Wellesley College and her MFA from the University of Virginia. Her first collection of poetry, *White Elephants* (Beacon Press, 1996), won the Barnard New Women Poets Prize, while her second collection, *World Hotel* (Copper Canyon Press, 2002), won the 2003 Anisfield-Wolf Book Award. Vazirani has also received a Pushcart Prize, a Poets and Writers exchange program award, the Glenna Luchei award from *Prairie Schooner,* a "Discovery"/*The Nation* award, and fellowships from the Bread Loaf and Sewanee Writers' conferences. A contributing and advisory editor for *Shenandoah,* she was the writer-in-residence at Sweet Briar College and later at the College of William and Mary. Vazirani died in 2003. Her posthumous collection, *Radha Says,* edited by Leslie McGrath and Ravi Shankar, was published by Drunken Boat Media in 2009.

It's a Young Country

and we cannot bear to grow old
James Baldwin   Marilyn Monroe
Marvin Gaye sing the anthem
at the next Superbowl
We say *America you are*
magnificent   and we mean
we are heartbroken
What fun we chase after it
Can't hurry go the Supremes
Next that diva soprano
for whom stagehands at the Met
wore the T-shirt *I Survived the Battle*

We leave for a better job
cross the frontier   *wish you*
were here in this hotel   Two of us one
we are with John Keats on his cot

in the lone dictionary I'm falling
on dilemma's two horns
If you are seducing another
teach me to share you with humor
Water in my bones and the sound
of a midnight telephone   *Hello love*
I am coming   I do not know
where you sleep   are you alone

We grow old   look at this
country its worn dungarees
picking cotton dredging ditches
stealing timber bullets prairies
America's hard work have mercy
in order to form a more perfect
some step forward some step back
neighbor here's a seat at my table
through orange portals lit tunnels
over bridges Brooklyn Golden Gate
weather be bright wheels turn yes
pack lightly we move so fast

From the Postcard at Vertigo Bookstore in D.C.

In the photograph of Billie Holiday at the 1957 Newport Jazz Festival, she
wears a low-cut evening gown and fawn-colored stole. Her rhinestone earrings
are shoulder-dusters, and her necklace falls almost to her cleavage in leaves
of glass stones, or maybe they are real. The bracelet on her wrist spans wide
as a man's shirt cuff, and her nails are frosted. The cigarette comes out at you,
foreshortened over a score where notes are few with wide spaces between . . .
Her hairline is even as Nefertiti's, eyebrows painted on with confidence, and
her lips, most likely red, are round in generous laughter for the photographer.
She is not singing: that was before, or she's going on later. Billie Holiday is
chic on her break; and when women open little drawers of half-used lipsticks
two shades off, and mascaras bought in anticipation, they know as I do looking
at my stash of glamor—we look for it and it's not there

It's Me, I'm Not Home

It's late in the city and I'm asleep.
You will call again? Did I hear
(please leave a message after the beep)

Chekhov? A loves B. I clap
for joy. B loves C. C won't answer.
In the city, it's late, I'm asleep,

and if your face nears me like a familiar map
of homelessness: old world, new hemisphere
(it's me leave a message after the beep),

then romance flies in the final lap
of the relay, I pass the baton you disappear
into the city, it's late and I'm asleep

with marriages again, they tend to drop
by, faithful to us for about a year,
leave a message after the beep,

I'll leave a key for you, play the tape
when you come in, or pick up the receiver.
It's late in the city and I'm asleep.
Please leave a message after the beep.

Aerogram Punjab

We sailed by Africa, back home.
You're good with maps; to find me
first find you in your atlas, your page,
not a tropic, a dashed line—
where did the whale go? Find
the page black. *Chota bhai,* tell me

where the world goes. Are you sledding
to the Lincoln Memorial, brother, tell me.
You're seven. Can you read *New Delhi*?

Say hello to Daddy for me. The tailor
made you a red kemize. Nude, every
day my stomach grows. What else—

sari never changes its size; our tailor's
discount. I have grown. What ails
me? Maybe it's a girl, my dowry-

free holiday. I'm a globe.
Some say a boy. I doubt it—
she moves like the ocean,

and the globe feels tighter.
Sail to Africa, to India.
She's not Asian.
You're good with maps. Find me.

VANDANA KHANNA

Vandana Khanna was born in New Delhi, India, and raised in the United States. She attended the University of Virginia and received her MFA from Indiana University in Bloomington, where she was a recipient of the Yellen Fellowship in poetry. Her collection of poetry, *Train to Agra,* won the 2000 *Crab Orchard Review* First Book Prize. Khanna's work has been nominated for a Pushcart Prize and has appeared in such journals as *Crazyhorse, Callaloo,* and the *Indiana Review,* as well as the anthologies *Homage to Vallejo* (Greenhouse Review Press, 2006) and *Asian American Poetry: The Next Generation* (Illinois University Press, 2004). She is currently working on her second collection of poetry, entitled *The Masala of the Afternoon,* which explores the connections among Indian cinema, food, and the immigrant experience. Khanna lives in Los Angeles, with her husband and three children.

> *I'm a Punjabi Virginian who spent childhood summers in Delhi,*
> *watched Bollywood films in the suburbs of D.C., and now makes a*
> *home in Hollywood.*

Blackwater Fever

They didn't find it in me until months later—
just like Vallejo who died on a rainy
day far from the heat rising over a garden
in silvers and reds—far away from the din
of buses, tobacco vendors, cows that overran
the streets with their holiness. Laid on the surface
of the Ganges, the thin shells reflected light, clamored
against the current. Far from the Atlantic, farther still
from the Potomac. Same color of night, dull dawn.
The fever should have churned my blood into tight
fists while the sunset stretched across the sky
like an open mouth. Everything was splintered heat.
I'd awake to winter in D.C., find streets covered
in snow, the words of some ancient language blooming

under my ankles like a song, a mantra called home.
I could trace it like a geography of someone I had once been.
How to explain the hum of mosquitoes in my ear, sensual
and low, nothing like the sound of rusted-out engines,
police sirens, a train's whistle. How easily I'd lost the taste
for that water, opened my legs to their hot, biting mouths.

Hair

Always the sound of knots tearing,
the scratch of hair against metal.
Those summer evenings when I'd go by

Anu's apartment on the floor above mine,
#406, and watch her mother tug at her hair
with a steel-toothed comb, their room

smelled of coconut oil and meat
left over from dinner. She can't cut it—ever.
And so, every night is a tug of war

with her mother, whose brown fingers
pull and rub, spreading it out like a sheet
against her back. Anu's father would laugh

at my skin, telling me to drink black tea,
sit in the sun, darken up, and let my hair grow
beyond my nape at least, his fingers

at the edge of my shirt collar. He'd never felt
the edges of a scissors' blade—his full gray beard
and hair mixing in a weave of silver-black—

a patchwork, a lifetime of wants, which he rolled
around the perimeter of his head and chin,
ending in a tight fist at the top. Her mother

whispered words into Anu's scalp and neck,
with each strand, a different story—of American boys
and dances, where skin touched, hair swayed

down backs, of the mythic Sita walking into fire
to prove her purity. We knew about American boys—
how there were none in our neighborhood,

how they'd ride by on bikes, and we'd watch them
from our bedroom windows and sometimes
from the front steps—their clean-skinned cheekbones,

smooth chests. All the while, Anu would move between
her mother's thighs like the fireflies we'd catch
in pickle jars, clicking and igniting in glass.

Dot Head

They caught us once between
the cypress trees, a block
from our apartment complex where

the hallways always smelled of beer
and boiled rice; though I don't remember
exactly, just two boys on bikes, the flash

of sunlight on steel handlebars, words
sharp, and the bite of mosquitoes
that burned our ankles. Something hard

hit my brother in the head. A red *bindi*
in the center of the forehead like a rose,
like the one I saw my mother wear, but

his bled down his face. A dot head,
a sand nigger—one of them who never
freckled during recess, smelled of curry

and spices, ate their sandwiches rolled up
in brown bread, skin dark as almonds.
Except they got it wrong. No matter how

many times they rode by, chasing us
with words, with rocks and broken bottles
spitting at our backs, they got it wrong.

It was a sign of being blessed after temple,
of celebration when women wore them, red-gold
to match silver-threaded saris, to match red and green

glass bangles that shivered up their forearms, my brother's
jagged, glittering more than a pundit's thumbprint,
more than a holy mark, glittering.

Echo

I cannot make it lovely,
this story of my father: his body
raw under the lights like a skinned

almond, surrounded by sandalwood,
pickled carrots, and the hush
of rice settling in a bag.

I can't help it, I need metaphors:
his body curls like the curve of a cheek,
a knife lies beside him, done with its work.

This story in metaphors. Not simply:
You lie on the floor. You've been cut
by two men you don't know. They wanted

money and you were too slow, didn't understand.
But rather: bruises braid his skin, the bitter black
of leaves, eyes red as the swollen sting

of chili powder. *Why do I write in the past?*
He smells only sweat, sickened blood seeping,
nothing familiar—not black and red pepper pinched

into the air, not the jasmine of his mother's
kitchen. Nothing—until his breath is like a tea
bag twisted, pressed into the cup of the room.

But it's not an Indian grocery, it is a shabby
downtown hotel, the kind that lock their doors
at ten, have security guards to stop the prostitutes

from coming in, from warming themselves
in the lobby. The kind where hallways echo
of accents. The phone is off the hook.

Not, *why do I write about the past?* but, *what story
must I tell?* You lie there dreaming, but I'm
not sure, dreaming of your childhood in Lahore:

the city escaping the finite lines of a map, erased
by riots, civil war. You remember the hot nights,
chattering birds—how the world was never silent then.

You tell me over and over but I can't write it:
the same story, but I know we are leaving
things out. Embellishing. What they must

have said, the words, harsh like Bengali, you never
tell, the first cut and then the next, how you fell
like a sack of mangoes into a heavy tumble.

You have left the spaces empty for me to add
in colors, the smells, to translate to English.
To translate into the present, into beautiful.

MOHAMMAD FAISAL HADI

Mohammad Faisal Hadi was born in Albany Park, Chicago, after his family emigrated from Hyderabad, India, in the 1970s. He is a graduate of the University of Illinois at Urbana-Champaign, where he first began writing poetry and where he was awarded the Art Blevins Prize for his narrative verse. He is a public school teacher who is actively involved with Asian American arts groups and nonprofit immigrant community projects in the Chicago area.

A second-generation South Asian American, my earliest memory of poetry is of my family's Urdu shayari.

My Uncle, Failing to Slaughter the Goat of His 12th Eid

You shine the blade against the morning moon, with clouds of sting-ray skin.
    With vinegar
you clean sickle sheen left from cutting hedges and vines from the tree,
    the grass from the lot.
You square shoulders, tighten stomach, swallow fear,
    like lye
bleaching thought. They're waiting in the yard as before, the year past,
    the uncles, the grandfathers, who never leave.

In the yard a dusty goat is caught up in the bramble of their rusty arms.
    The buck's head tilts
towards you, its sweet breath mixed with manure,
    its brown eyes
filled with the docile memory of carrots and turnips,
    already hungry.
They place a trough beneath, push down its haunches,
    call you forward.

You go down. You are for the first time conscious of your gait.
    Forgetting your walk

you stumble. Women peer down in nightclothes
        from curtained windows.
You swing the weight of the hilt. You feel the juncture of blade and handle,
        earth and haunch,
handle and pommel, knob worked with fine dents, dimpled and reflective,
        casting back

from hand hammered dints of bronze, tiny visions.
        You see yourself:
a thousand different postures, a thousand lives, walking through a thousand
        narrow gullies.
One leads away. You take it slowly, pivoting. You turn
        lowering blade to animal
to one silver bristled ear, drawing it bloodlessly
        in slow caress

you turn from the toothless laughter of old men, from women
        leaning from screenless windows,
begin to walk the brick path through the garden, past chameli shrubs,
        then into the stink of the street.
You turn the pommel in your hand, upending fates. You walk backwards
        into a new land.

Fatima

from fear to isolation
never leaving the apartment
for weeks the neighbors
repeating your name in the
hallways your children on
the phone in distant cities
entombed in television glow
until the last bag the last
can the last sickly sprig
of parsley and down the
steps head covered but not

veiled head covered though
you thought twice this time
the first time you had to
think and see hard your
block the fruit market
the laundry the church the
bank the masjid the police
the school the temple see
hard the cracks in the
sidewalk the look of it all
the dust on everything

Public Benefits

We come with plastic bags,
culled from the local grocery,
nude, white, green, grey,
a supermarket logo wrapped round
envelopes, torn open jagged with a finger,
letters just arrived from city offices,
the county,
from social security,
from the police,
from immigration,
departments of justice,
the telephone company,
the emergency room,
from the institutes and courts and ledgers
erected in testimony to the countless
births, deaths, and marriages
that bookend our lives,
these lives, stretched now,
condensed and reconstituted,
across oceans and ration-lines.

We stretch back nylon skin,
dislodge passports and visas,
documents tender as cotton,
folded and refolded like handkerchiefs,
hospital patient cards
stamped like dog-tags.

On spotted counter-tops,
after standing for three hours
in the desert of a food-stamp intake line,
amidst mountains of manila folders,
pronged with tin-teeth,
in drifts of Medicaid cards,
before thankless glances,
eyeless and distant,
we stack the evidence,
are asked to repeat ourselves and
translate for others,
pile bits of paper,
conjure our existence,
to prop open the jaws of life.

MAYA KHOSLA

Maya Khosla received the Dorothy Brunsman Poetry Prize for her first poetry collection, *Keel Bone* (Bear Star Press, 2003). Her other publications include a chapbook of poetry, *Heart of the Tearing* (Red Dust Press, 1996), and a collection of nonfiction, *Web of Water* (Golden Gate National Park Association, 1997). Her poems have appeared in the *Wisconsin Review,* the *Seneca Review,* the *New Orleans Review,* the *Literary Review,* and *Permafrost,* and she has received the Ludwig Vogelstein Award and residencies from the Headlands Center for the Arts and the Sanskriti Foundation in New Delhi. Having lived in Bangladesh, Burma, Bhutan, England, India, and several places in the United States, she now works as a consultant in biology and toxicology in California. She has just completed her second collection of poetry, *Clingstone* (working title).

> *Having worked in rivers with runs of migratory fish, I think of my*
> *own Indian identity in terms of a homing instinct that defines my*
> *writing by the virtue of its specific current.*

Oppenheimer quotes *The Bhagavad Gita*

> The atomic energy commission formulated its research policy in
> a series of meetings,
> the most important one held at Bohemian Grove . . .

I want to walk this new land.
Twisted iron. Fine, cream-colored dust
covers everything, the slippers I slip into.
They are melted together
like a woman's wrist bones.
I did not ask to look.
But she lives in the umbra of silence
beseeching me, stump-arms lifted.

It has been years
since the night-clad car pulled up
alongside my stride.
I was barefoot, a refugee
with physics under one arm.

I was escorted to where tall redwoods
spoke with their thousand-year breath.
I wanted to listen to their story
of quiet moisture and verve—

but human voices swelled in crescendo,
begging me for molecular secrets,
for the white heat of light.
The redwoods swayed, turned skyward

as I do now. Rain pelts, fast and gritty,
turns ashen. Around me, faces, wet faces
so tranquil I could swear
it isn't blood, but just sleep,
dripping from their mouths.

Now wind, my upturned umbrella:
ribs displaying themselves, open, captive,
under thick cloud-jaws.
Brighter than a thousand suns
I am become death, destroyer of the worlds.

I find water, drink. It lights up,
a fiery eye scorching sleep.

Return to Grand Canyon

> We occupy one moment, that's all. And as I say "this moment"
> it's gone.
>
> —Gouri Khosla

You craved the canyon music.
So I return. It takes years
to slice your words open—
juices dripping—to swallow all
but the slippery seeds,
which will take a journey
and a lingering season
to sow. I know
to leave my watch behind,

to cache the seeds, my pockets bulging,
and track their habitat
past cities glittering with glass,
shingles, and spare change,
past rivers of fake white light,
down miles of desert trails
honeyed by the breathy heat
of ceanothus, cactus buds
their water held, private as moons.

Salt cakes my cheeks and neck,
working a good thirst, seeking
the right loam.
With each step, the tongue
of my backpack buckle
rings like a temple bell
inside a steel cup on my back.

This moment. I track it
through a thick

and brittle-barked country,
pink dust-miles covering my shoes.
At dusk, the heat sinks beneath
redstone, touching crepuscular nerves
into emergence. Bats trill,
lace the windburn
with a pilgrimage of their own:
doubles of sound chirping back
from fiery canyon walls.

When the words grow half a mile
deep in rock
it's tricky finding their dispersal spot.
In fact, I almost pass it.
Tilt back for a sip, the first in miles,
and there they are overhead, frescoes,
songs without throat, blood-paint
on smoky boulders:
water, dragonfly, shadowy deer in flight.
I empty my pockets
into the great hush beneath.

Sequoia Sempervirens

The sequoias form a country of giant women
in conference, wrapped in dark shawls.

Saplings hover under grandmothers holding rain.
Their poise recalls silences before Aztec fires,

metal and meat. Descending the mountains
two hundred years ago, they cradled the bloody

remains, the chopped red bark of sisters,
swelling in stream corridors. Woody feet

linked under the earth. Their keening rose
in waves, drawing ferns, fog-oceans,

curtains of insects in. Now calm,
the women chop light into slivers, eat,

store chunk sugars in vertical rivers of xylem.
Flocks of ancient birds climb down ladders

of sun and bark. Harvest what crawls
the wood-ribbed hearts.

Under Wolf-Paw

You are telling me to leave.
That *you* couldn't break
the single file of parents, grandparents
who reaped wheat, watching each grain
drop through generations of waiting.
That you are brittlebush, stiff
entrenched too long and deep
under wolf-paw and snow
to shift, but you want me to take
the raw jaggery, the shoes,
to wake before the sky climbs,
and reach the border before light
twists and snaps through the cobwebs
under wild apricot trees.
Take what you can.
The gifts are delicate,
but your words click with the clout
of nail in leather. Tonight we are copper
and fire and old song, cupping cinnamon
steam to our faces, eyes on a distance
too dark to sing about

but rich enough to sip and smell,
while all around us the candles
are breathing slower than I am,
even in this cold. *Stay curled. Don't shoot*
your one green arm into the sun
until you get there. Go
with crow-claw to hunt the light.
Turn what you can into wings.

TANUJA MEHROTRA

Born in Cleveland, Ohio, Tanuja Mehrotra spent a couple of years in West Virginia before moving to Jacksonville, Florida, where she spent most of her childhood. She holds a BA from Wellesley College, an MA in English from Tulane University, and an MFA in creative writing from San Francisco State University. Mehrotra has been awarded the Academy of American Poets Prize and the Amanda Sterner Butler Prize for poetry. Her poems have appeared in the *Asian Pacific American Journal, Transfer, Dogwood,* and the *Fourteen Hills Review.* Currently, she is working on her first collection of poetry, a book based on her invented form of "threaded ghazals." She lives with her husband and two young daughters in Belmont, California.

I'm an Indian American living in California who sings to my daughters of a childhood spent in Florida.

Manthara

she scatters the deck of cards as if she were the wind
but the cards cling to each other in defiance

her cheeks puff purple as she blows harder
a thousand icicle tips melt on our skin

sputters wee and whoa when she walks
wheezing and whistling through her bones

the courtyard smells of her breath
sends sugar swimming in our mouths

her howls lick our faces with a rough tongue
it is what we expect

from the hump-back, from Manthara
scratching the sandstone of Ayodhya

whispering into squirming children's ears
the cards won't always stay safely stacked

open windows beckon the monsoons
to blanket the palace tiles in moisture

she raves at us to wipe them dry until the blood
from our fingers stains the white floor carnelian

our life is just the hand we are dealt by God
but Manthara, fists clenched, rocks her imagined princess to sleep

carpets of revenge and jealousy, we beat out over the terrace
dust drifts down into the river that flows like petrified wood

she drowns herself daily in its water
cleanses herself with bark—termites nibble her hair

we hear her toothless prayers every morning
caress the beads of holiness in her hands

from the river bank we listen for the mumbling
tale to tell our servant children, tale to tell theirs

remember the woman whose shrunken, stone-filled
story sags and tears the cloth it is held in

a tale to rip open, caress those stones spilling
into cupped hands, then we will understand

the deck of cards laugh into the breeze
and call on God's expert hand to scoop them up, shuffle, deal again

Nainital

a sestina

See how an August rain falls on Lake Naini.
How it has changed so! Like the Capitol Cinema—
once freshly painted white with a roof of brilliant red.
We could spy the red from our school in the hills,
and between final period and dinner in the mess, sneak in a film
and from the comic shop sample Cadbury chocolates.

Collecting in our pockets so many Cadbury chocolates,
we spent our spare hours rowing boats on the lake.
Or if by some off chance we did not want to see a film,
we leaned against the stone balustrade outside Capitol Cinema,
watching silhouetted figures import the samba and the fox-trot to the hills,
their shadows dancing in the clubhouse whose roof was also red.

The insignia on our Biryla Mundir uniforms was not sewn in red
but in gold and purple like the candy wrappers of the Cadbury chocolates
we littered along the steep pathways through the hills.
Hills rise on all sides around Lake Naini.
Near the flats, beside the lake, rests Capitol Cinema
where I saw all the musicals—my introduction to film!

An American in Paris . . . Suddenly Last Summer . . . we watched only western
    films;
Elizabeth Taylor in a sleek, silk dress that must have been red,
although the film was in black and white at the Capitol Cinema.
Before each film, we stopped at the comic shop for the Cadbury chocolates,
which I purchased for everyone since my father made himself known in
    Lake Naini.
He told the shopkeeper, "Keep a tab for this boy, my son, who studies there,
    in those hills."

He pointed and the shopkeeper nodded, for all the boarding schools were
    in the hills.

My father did not know how much I loved to take in a film
at the cinema house towering on the shore of Lake Naini.
Since the bills came to him of so many rupees marked in red,
he did know how much I adored those Cadbury chocolates.
Chocolates we gobbled in the dark while gazing at the lit-up screen of the
  Capitol Cinema.

How I found refuge in that Capitol Cinema!
Free from the heavy chemistry textbooks awaiting me in the hills!
How can I make you see that roof of vibrant, blood-beating red?
Faded now! Reproducible, perhaps, in a film.
All in the past, what I loved of Lake Naini.
Impossible to see what it was or taste it even in a square of Cadbury chocolate.

I might use a filter tinted with red, if I made a film,
and open the scene with an aerial shot of Capitol Cinema from the hills.
I might say: this is the lake, Lake Naini, Nainital, where I first tried Cadbury
  chocolates.

Song for New Orleans

>   Sitting still in New Orleans
>   The wet, hot fill of New Orleans

from an attic apartment, I watch the neighbor's gutted roof. it gapes at the sky.
watch pigeon after pigeon fly through that roof. the house of pigeon midwifery.

Armand
He's tired
So tired
But he can't sleep

a live oak cracks open the sidewalk, roots fit to burst through concrete dancing to a fiddledeedee funkadelic song

the mardi gras indian stretches his feathered wings

he preens for our eyes to feast

> A district, a parish, a ward. A tourist, a
> tossed sugar pie. The trill in New Orleans

Armand
He's tired
So, so tired
But he will not sleep

> He watches thru the window
> Bluebird on a willow
> Daylight fades to yellow
> But his eyes yearn green

> Birds on the windowsill taunt him
> His soft paw bats the window trim
> These days, he says, these days are grim
> With many more to see

beads beads beads. purple, gold, green. rear-ending a meter maid on Milan
(say it My-lan) street or was it Tchoupitoulas?

Armand is tired
So, so tired
But he will not sleep

The window grows colder
That bluebird sings bolder
Armand's bones groan older
How he longs to fly free

                              Gravestones sweat above ground, stone
                              angels embrace their kill in New Orleans

wading into a street of water up to my thighs trying to get the car out alive

the ferrets, beezus and ramona, they loved to be bathed

wilting on the edges of a quarter

            Feline dream life, I can tell,
            Is deeper than a wishing well
            Richer than this mortal hell
            Hanging from a tree

                              He chews slowly, surely he chews at the hot dog
                              bits laid bare on a windowsill in New Orleans

"But you have fleas! People had fleas!" he shouts at the girl grossed out by
    Donne's conceit.

professor ray extends a hankie, a guitar, a song once sung by Fred Astaire.

it's never what we say, is it? it's how we say it. to whom we say it.

to earn a living at brightness

Armand, I'll give you birds at sea
You do not need to comfort me
Window is open, can't you see
Feathers in the breeze

An orange offered moments before she dies
a glowing orb of birds sing shrill in New Orleans

the dark black woman in a pink antebellum gown gives us a tour of the
   plantation

gestures toward the servant quarters

glass bulbs with honey to catch the flies

professor maddy tells us a victorian scholar (in this very department,
   someone we know) purposely killed her corgi

"That conference was the first time I went someplace without Daddy. I was
eating in a hotel and I saw they had Irish coffee. I thought of back home
with condensed milk and lots of sugar. But this. It had a different taste. I
could barely open my eyes the next morning. But I've changed. I like that
Asti Spumanti. And the Margarita wine coolers. Those are really nice!"

annotated bibliographies

how proudly he claimed his ear was tin

to eat beignets, to garden, to meditate, to do anything other than hunt for
   traces of empire in "To Autumn"

A quarter. An antique. The wrought iron of a fence
the levee drinks, a hollowing hill in New Orleans

Armand, he's tired
So, so tired
When will he sleep?

Dad and I stand for an hour inside that sound. Preservation of jazz, tang of
piano and slow trombone, whirring fans. We watch the instruments talk to
each other in the heat, wooden floorboards catching all that falls away. Step
into the night and Daddy says, "My God. My, my. Let's eat this ice cream."

VIJAY SESHADRI

Vijay Seshadri is the author of *Wild Kingdom* (1996) and *The Long Meadow* (2004), both from Graywolf Press. His poems, essays, and reviews have been published in *AGNI*, the *American Scholar*, *Antaeus*, the *Nation*, the *New Yorker*, the *Paris Review*, *Shenandoah*, the *Southwest Review*, the *Threepenny Review*, *Verse*, the *Western Humanities Review*, the *Yale Review*, the *New York Times Book Review*, and *TriQuarterly*, and in anthologies such as *Under 35: The New Generation of American Poets*, *The Anchor Essay Annual*, *Best American Poetry* (1997, 2003, and 2006), and Best Creative Nonfiction (2008). Seshadri's awards include the *Paris Review*'s Bernard F. Conners Long Poem Prize, the MacDowell Colony's Fellowship for Distinguished Poetic Achievement, and the Academy of American Poets James Laughlin Prize, as well as grants from the NEA and the John Simon Guggenheim Memorial Foundation. Born in Bangalore, India, in 1954, Seshadri came to America at the age of five. He lives in Brooklyn and teaches at Sarah Lawrence College.

> *I like being many different things and am grateful to history for*
> *opening the doors to so many different worlds and peoples to me.*

The Disappearances

"Where was it one first heard of the truth?"

On a day like any other day,
like "yesterday or centuries before,"
in a town with the one remembered street,
shaded by the buckeye and the sycamore—
the street long and true as a theorem,
the day like yesterday or the day before,
the street you walked down centuries before—
the story the same as the others flooding in
from the cardinal points is

turning to take a good look at you.
Every creature, intelligent or not, has disappeared—
the humans, phosphorescent,
the duplicating pets, the guppies and spaniels,
the Woolworth's turtle that cost forty-nine cents
(with the soiled price tag half-peeled on its shell)—
but from the look of things, it only just happened.
The wheels of the upside-down tricycle are spinning.
The swings are empty but swinging.
And the shadow is still there, and there
is the object that made it,
riding the proximate atmosphere,
oblong and illustrious above
the dispeopled bedroom community,
venting the memories of those it took,
their corrosive human element.
This is what you have to walk through to escape,
transparent but alive as coal dust.
This is what you have to hack through,
bamboo-tough and thickly clustered.
The myths are somewhere else, but here are the meanings,
and you have to breathe them in
until they burn your throat
and peck at your brain with their intoxicated teeth.
This is you as seen by them, from the corner of an eye
(was that the way you were always seen?).
This is you when the President died
(the day is brilliant and cold).
This is you poking a ground-wasps' nest.
This is you at the doorway, unobserved,
while your aunts and uncles keen over the body.
This is your first river, your first planetarium, your first popsicle.
The cold and brilliant day in six-color prints—
but the people on the screen are black and white.
Your friend's mother is saying,
Hush, children! Don't you understand history is being made?

You do, and you still do. Made and made again.
This is you as seen by them, and them as seen by you,
and you as seen by you, in five dimensions,
in seven, in three again, then two,
then reduced to a dimensionless point
in a universe where the only constant is the speed of light.
This is you at the speed of light.

Elegy

I've been asked to instruct you about the town you've gone to,
where I've never been.
The cathedral is worth looking at,
but the streets are narrow, uneven, and a little grim.
The river is sluggish in the summer and muddy in the spring.
The cottage industries are obsolete.
The population numbers one.

The population numbers one fugitive
who slips into the shadows and haunts the belfries.
His half-eaten meals are cold on the empty café tables.
His page of unsolved equations is blowing down the cobblestones.
His death was so unjust that he can't forgive himself.
He waits for his life to catch up to him.

He is you and you and you.
You will look to him for your expiation,
face him in the revolving door, sit with him in the plaza
and soothe his fears and sympathize with his story
and accustom him to the overwhelming sun
until his death becomes your death.
You will restore his confiscated minutes to him one by one.

The Dream I Didn't Have

I woke up on the stainless-steel autopsy table.
My chest was weighted down.
Bodily fluids stained my paper hospital gown.
My life readings were stable,

though. They were, in fact, decisive—
one round number and one simple line.
A cop gave the coroner a form to sign,
but he lingered undecided over me,

murmuring to himself,
"That must have been a dream, or was it a vision?"
I felt along my length his long riverine incision.
Outside it was Chicago—

city of world-class museums,
handsome architecture, marvelous elevated trains—
rising from the plains
by the impossibly flat lake.

Memoir

Orwell says somewhere that no one ever writes the real story of their life.
The real story of a life is the story of its humiliations.
If I wrote that story now—
radioactive to the end of time—
people, I swear, your eyes would fall out, you couldn't peel
the gloves fast enough
from your hands scorched by the firestorms of that shame.
Your poor hands. Your poor eyes
to see me weeping in my room
or boring the tall blonde to death.
Once I accused the innocent.
Once I bowed and prayed to the guilty.

I still wince at what I once said to the devastated widow.
And one October afternoon, under a locust tree
whose blackened pods were falling and making
illuminating patterns on the pathway,
I was seized by joy,
and someone saw me there,
and that was the worst of all,
lacerating and unforgettable.

BHANU KAPIL

Bhanu Kapil has written three full-length prose/poetry works: *The Vertical Interrogation of Strangers* (Kelsey Street Press, 2001), *Incubation: A Space for Monsters* (Leon Works, 2006), and *Humanimal, a Project for Future Children* (Kelsey Street Press, 2009). She lives in Colorado, where she teaches writing in the year-round program at Naropa University and at Goddard College, as part of its low-residency MFA program. Her current projects are a work of fiction, "Chimp Haven," an Orwellian take on chimpanzee rehabilitation on the border of Louisiana and Texas, and "Schizophrene," a creative nonfiction work that examines themes of migration and mental illness, in their intersection with race and domestic violence, in the Indian and Pakistani communities of northwest London. Kapil also maintains the blog "Was Jack Kerouac a Punjabi? A Day in the Life of a Naropa University Writing Professor."

I am a British (and newly U.S.) citizen, born to Indian (Punjabi)
parents in the UK in 1968.

from *Humanimal [a project for future children]*

15. Coming over a ridge, Joseph saw two pale animals, their
heads hanging down and thick with brown dreadlocks. They
were drinking from a river with a pack of wolves. A twig
snapped underfoot as Joseph strained to look but at that
moment, the animals fled, in one sharp curve, back into the
green. At night, the animals came once again to drink. In
his hide, Joseph shivered. He could not see them clearly but
he knew they were there. In the moonlight, the wolves and
their companions were whitish, with eyes that shone when
they turned towards him, mildly, reflexively. Blue.

g. Wet, wet, green, green. I mix with them and
prosper. Sticky then my mother licks me clean.
The nest is brown. Best is brown next to yellow.

Best is blue then brown. Best yellow. Where will
the sun go when it is finished? I ask my mother.
I put my lips against her skin and drink. Her milk
is white and then the sun goes in the ground. Because
my mother does, she does so every night.
We watch her disappear and then we disappear.
Blue as blue then brown then green then black.

16.i. In the bedroom, he tried to feed her with a copper
spoon, a mineralized utensil to replenish her blood. He
made her eat, watching the pink food—a kind of semolina
pudding mixed with jam—pool in her mouth. Her mouth
was an O and with his fingers he tried to press her gums
and teeth together. "*Eat.*" In the time I am writing of, villagers
from the settlement of Midnapure came regularly to
the orphanage, lining up at the gate to catch a glimpse of
the two jungle children. For a few minutes a day, Joseph's
wife, the Home's Mother, let them in and they swarmed
to the room where the youngest girl was failing. They
watched her fade and jerk in her cot, the spittle coming
down over her chin. From these stories, I constructed an image
of the dying girl as larval; perennially white, damp and
fluttering in the darkness of the room.

16.ii. "She was buried in the churchyard of St. John's Church,
Midnapure, on the twenty-first of September, 1921. Her
death certificate ran as follows: This is to certify that Amala
(wolf-child), a girl of the Rev. Singh's Orphanage, died of nephritis
on September 21, 1921. She was under my treatment.
September 21, 1921. sd/-s.p. Sabadhicari. Indian Medical
Service."—Joseph Singh.

16.iii. In Midnapure, I met the grandson of Dr. Sabadhicari.
As the film-makers asked him to describe the stories his
grandfather had told him, I sketched, in my notebook, the
emerald green, rusted spiral staircase partially illuminated

in the dark hallway behind him. Suspicious of our cameras,
Dr. Sabadhicari retold the tale his grandfather had told him,
of the two feral children, from the front step of his door.
"What is this for? Are you American?"

17. I substitute images for events, my humanimal prerogative.
Thus, here are the legs, wrapped in cotton wool to prevent
them from breaking; for the shocks absorbed in transport,
in the act of getting here at all.

18. A doctor came from Midnapure with a vial of herbal medicine
and a knife. Wizardly, grandmother-like, he stuck out
his chest and stomach and said: "Where are they?" The
girls. The doctor strung a knife above the cot where one girl
lay on the white sheet. Her face was wet. The cook soaked
the water up with a square of cotton and the Father backed
out of the room. In the garden, the sky hung down in violet
sections like a torn net and the Father stood there, beneath
it, calling out to the angels in their dominion. When
the youngest girl died, the doctor came out into the garden
and sank into a wicker chair. It was a chair from Nepal, the
edge of the region. The Mother brought the doctor a plate
of buttered chicken and chilies, which he ate quickly and
sloppily, like a dog.

VIKAS MENON

Born in Ohio and raised in Pennsylvania, Vikas Menon received his MFA in poetry from Brooklyn College and his MA in literature from St. Louis University. His poems have appeared in *Bitter Oleander, Catamaran,* the *Literary Review,* the *New Delta Review, MIPOESIAS,* the *Toronto Review,* and *TriQuarterly.* Menon was a finalist in the Writers at Work competition, and his first play, *Lead with Your Left,* was produced at the South Asian Theatre Arts Guild Experiment's (STAGE) One Act Festival in Washington, D.C. He is a board member of Kundiman, an organization dedicated to cultivating Asian American poetry, and the literary manager of the Ruffled Feathers theater company. Menon currently lives in New York City, where he is a grant writer for a health and human services agency. He recently completed work on his first collection of poetry, *godflesh.*

> *While I identify as South Asian American, my family has its roots in Kerala and speaks Malayalam, and I have a strong kinship with that particular South Indian culture and ethnicity.*

Radha

Let the nailmarks Radha makes remove your pain. . . .

—Vakpati

Refracted in sidewinder
crashes of subway
steel, swallowed
by the metal coils
of an endless electric
naga, jaws shut behind me,

and I stand, staring away from her.

The Dark God has stuffed
my mouth with silk
                        I wonder of her smell
              the scent of her inner thigh
                        count the creases behind her knees

              I shut my eyes

Like Him, I too had dropped from between a woman's legs,
bloodslick blue,
first breath a wail, mouths
greedy at breast, smashing pots with a chubby tantrum fist.

Yet I want to lay down
                        —sheets knotted and tangled—
              —tongue furred with her—
like Vasudeva

              clasped
      between Radha's fierce thighs

                        her prayer sharp flame.

I feel her narrow stare,

              she, who had strapped his sweatsoaked body
              to the wheel of birth and rebirth, she, silts of silver

              beached in the black tangle of her hair, Ekalavya's
              thumb strung on black string around her neck,
              she pulls the bowstring taut against her cheek:

Kesava's foot bobs like a deer mouthing grass

> she kneels beside his body
> touches kajal
> around his eyes

> elsewhere,
> a foal took its first stilting

steps

Drown

However and wherever
you find the god, bring him back to us.
Bring him back,
but first tell him,

tell him that the love
of his life is dead, and will rot
before he arrives back
to our arms.

He will cripple, be dung-laden
hobble on frail bones.
He will lose all his hair.
He will arrive like us:
spitting water from his mouth.

Urdu Funk: The Gentle Art of Subtitles

the lover must remove the veil
of her face. hell will
fall if papa hears him. if the storm of disgrace
enters through the window,
my father's turban will be disrespected.
don't develop an affair with
me. this is the dust of the storm in your
eyes which can cause havoc.
truth is always dry.

SUMMI KAIPA

Summi Kaipa received her MFA from the Iowa Writers' Workshop. She is the author of three chapbooks of poetry, *The Epics* (Leroy, 1999), *I Beg You Be Still* (Belladonna, 2003), and *The Language Parable* (Corollary Press, 2006). Her work has been published in *Chain, XCP: Cross Cultural Poetics,* the *Literary Review,* and the anthology *Bay Poetics* (Faux Press, 2006). She received the Holmes Award from the *Fourteen Hills Review* and the Potrero Nuevo Fund Prize in 2002 for her first play. From 1998 to 2003, Kaipa was also the founder and editor of *Interlope,* a magazine featuring experimental writing by Asian Americans, and was a literary curator for the Alliance of Emerging Creative Artists and New Langton Arts. Kaipa recently earned her doctorate in psychology and is completing her first full-length collection of poetry. She lives with her husband in Berkeley, California.

> *While finding kinship in being South Asian and Desi, I am also a Telugu Californian with an Arkansas past.*

from *A Personal Cinema*

Qurbani

"Hi, Lollipop!" catcalls the horny matron. As Firoz Khan turns around to look at her, we witness his winsome profile. He's a cross between the bumbling Mr. Bean and the unswervingly suave Pierce Brosnan. His Solid Gold girlfriend sports shimmery floor length dresses and sings lounge songs with backup girls like Abba in space-age silver go-go boots. I wished I was Zeenat Aman, the Indian Bo Derek "10," and dreamed of her white feather boas to wrap around my shoulders while I mimicked her shaking hips. The dulcet voices of my family sadly skipped past me like a tooth fairy forgetting a kid on her rounds. A motorcycle helmet in hand, Firoz Khan embodies cool and watches on. They are in love, or they are in love without kisses, which led most of us down a path of wonder and confusion. Were passionate "French" ones ever swapped by Indians? Or did they just dance and sing and fight in jeans that were too snug or a sweater a decade too ripe? But the curve of Zeenat's belly is precise, and her red sequined number all fever. Large circles of fabric missing where the hips of her dress should be. A hundred times, I pressed rewind, a carrot as my microphone, belting off-key "Aap Jaisa Koi . . ." with the disco sound of falling stars nevertheless egging me on. "Arre, Zeenat!" My father winked at the uncles, and Firoz, listening, drunk on a cocktail of lust, knows he's a lucky man.

Hare Rama Hare Krishna

After Jassbir, almost blind, loses her glasses, it's all downhill. Daddy's flirtations unzip the family unit. In a swift and untenable fork in the story, Mom and Prashant are gone. Dead? Something like that. Back then, the distance between continents like the suspension of disbelief in this story was insurmountable. The bold girl flips her hurt into a Kerouac karmic love and trades coke bottle glasses for glamorously large pink frames. I ditched mine, too, and got hip after slipping on the word "rhetoric" and losing the 8th grade spelling bee. A beaten up copy of *The Dharma Bums,* the one she borrowed from me, on her bedside table next to the painkillers and poppers. "What does the world care about us?" she sings, as she puffs at a pipe and raises her arm to the sky. When I first lost my religion, I sullenly dreamt of the rooftop parties on Rose Street and wondered, punch-drunk, if The Beats might help me find it. Flubbing chemistry and fingering poetry like a new charm, I hummed "Dum Maro Dum," with the image of Zeenat's backside like an hourglass ticking at the hip. Descent into hell, we're supposed to believe, is made easier by a corrupted Canadian background. Only the West can beget such exquisite womanly decadence, and I am filled with admiration and autobiography.

from *The Epics*

7.

Once born, the possibilities. Ambika's child: Blind Drthrastra—five consonants in a row tripping up the American tongue. Ambalika's: the fair haired, fair skinned Pandu is antecedent to the Pandavas. Let us not forget that there are other progressions that help the story along—that Satyavati begs Vyasa to try again with Ambika, but interference occurs in our television screens. The "current" goes due to the scheduled power outages, the bugs bite in the dark. We do not name ourselves Hindustanis but get named by the Persians as such. Vyasa in the room, awaiting Ambika for insemination, again—darkness does the job better. Deceiving the scruffy Brahmin, Ambalika encourages her maid servant in lieu of her. The translator notes: "Ruskin said of Shakespeare that he has no heroes but only heroines. In *The Mahabharata* there are many heroes: they may have their failings but they also rise to great heights. It is however, very difficult to find a true heroine in these pages." More likely than not, a woman enjoys being fondly known as a receptacle for brave sons and beautiful daughters with fertile wombs. In *Anandamath,* one of the first Indian "novels," appears the nationalist song (in opposition to British oppression) "Bande Mataram"—the nation becomes likened to mother, not woman. My multilinguality is a convenient apparatus though I once lied about being able to read Italian. (In some circles, Telugu is known as the "Italian of the East.") To the narrative: the faithful maid servant is not afraid of Vyasa, welcoming the unshaven Brahmin. Many early presidents lived in log cabins. We are prone to awarding bright people with lynching. Du Bois "the problem of the twentieth century is the problem of the color line" eventually expatriated. The maid servant, who goes unnamed, bears the brilliant Vidura. The lights are up, the television is inundated with commercials of Fair and Lovely skin cream and the ever-healing Zendu Balm. Mosquitoes rest on posters of Sonia Gandhi.

9.

The poet leaves out details. The poet writes and re-writes her version of *The Mahabharata* with next season's highlights. The poet jumps the gun (and loves it). M & D brought one suitcase with them. M, 19, shed her saris and went to work in a spark plug factory. I am telling a lie when I say that their first car was a Dodge Dart, but it begs to be part of the epic show. M, 20, is pregnant in Detroit, Michigan—where the Dart plows through the snow. Into the myth and no snow, we insert Kunti, Pandu's first wife, who can conjure a child on request and can just as easily trash her first born (& does). Everything happens for a reason—don't let anyone tell you how to play your 3-cards. Or we can draw a line on slate between fate and every event. (How P dies when he shoots a Brahmin couple who, in the form of courting deer, are in the middle of making love. But he doesn't die instantly. The angry Brahmin man immediately reveals himself incarnated human— though was he wearing clothes? No one knows.) Like in the Demi Moore–Patrick Swayze movie, *Ghost,* when Demi touches Whoopi Goldberg's hand—her fingernails painted bright red—and loves her (as Patrick Swayze), I couldn't suspend my disbelief. "Pandu, you will die whenever you attempt to touch your wife with lust." Kunti's away from the ruckus, all alone, like M who was pregnant at home, having quit her spark plug job. And Kunti's getting things done on her own—bringing five powerful boys, the Pandavas, into the world. M, in the hospital bed beside Kunti, births the kavi. The girl poet catapulted public. The poet's brother was stumbling into the furniture and stealing the microphone before he was even able to speak. The girl poet was learning the words to "Choodu Chinnama" while Sami swung his baby Elvis hips along—"Look, Auntie, the bad boy keeps threatening to jump from the top floor." While Yudhisthira, just born, was never to learn "you got to know when to hold 'em, know when to fold 'em," and Sami, D, and I sang along.

MINAL HAJRATWALA

Author of the nonfiction book *Leaving India: My Family's Journey from Five Villages to Five Continents* (Houghton Mifflin Harcourt, 2009), Minal Hajratwala is also a poet and performer. Her one-woman show, *Avatars: Gods for a New Millennium,* was commissioned by the Asian Art Museum of San Francisco in 1999. Her creative work has received recognition from the Sundance Institute, the Jon Sims Center for the Arts, the Serpent Source Foundation, and the Hedgebrook retreat for women writers, where she serves on the Alumnae Leadership Council. As a journalist, she worked at the *San Jose Mercury News* for eight years and was a National Arts Journalism Program fellow at Columbia University in 2000–2001. She is a graduate of Stanford University.

Identity as platform, not label. My identities include Gujarati, queer, diasporan, San Franciscan, poet, performer, writing coach, editor, recovering journalist, and more.

Angerfish

I.

On the first day
the fish wrapped in straw
starts to stink.

On the second day
if you walk by the barn
it enters your clothes.

That evening your wife
sniffs your suit
but says nothing.

On the third day
dressed in your skin
the fish begins to walk.

Your friends know
to hold their breaths.
This is not the first time.

If nothing else happens
the fish retreats
to its mean nest.

You shower.
It sleeps
waiting for you.

Fish oils
soak the hay
of the whole barn.

The chickens begin to dream
of seaweed,
of roe.

II.

In the middle of it
the fish
is the wisest
truest thing you know.

It whispers
sweet sauces—
We are brought here to love, yes,
but not blindly.

Its jelly eye
winks at you
codes of Morse—
No remorse.

Every oracle
takes its price,
skin for scales,
gold for gills.

Some days
it is a bargain.
Or else it costs
everything you have.

III.

I was raised without the fish
as some children are raised without candy
or time.

No one in my family spoke of it
as no one spoke then of cities
or queers.

Somehow in the cradle, rocking,
I caught a whiff; or in the crib clutching
at rails

a bit of fish caught
rough in my scream.
Swallow.

Since then the fish has grown in me
like bubblegum or seeds of water
melons.

Since then we're bosom tight
thick as thieves sealed with a
kiss—kin.

Is this what I meant
when I longed for teeth?
Is this what they meant

when they named me *fish?*
Soon I shall slit my
belly

to stroke its silver scales
bilious, slippery
as love.

IV.

At last the fish
swallows its own tail

scale by creamy scale
orgy of self-

righteous   lips
on sharp bone

tongue sucking spine
vertebra by vertebra

teeth shredding
gummy ovaries

ripe with black meat
millions of living

egg of fish.
Belly full of self

soft pulsing
heart of fish

parallel eyes
forehead

white gills
filled

with the last sea.
When the fish

is all jaw
row of incisors

grinding plankton
coral   salt

churning oceans
like milk

into sweet fat
gold

then I will be ready
for you.

. . . who "wrap up" anger—that is, wrap around [themselves] repeatedly
the anger based on the thought "he reviled me," and so on, like wrapping
up the pole of a cart with thongs, or putrid fish with straw—when enmity
arises in such persons, it is not appeased, pacified.

—*Dhammapada I.4*

Miss Indo-America dreams

Please send me, she says
Please send me a banner
to lift and separate my gifts
Please send me an agent
a Bollywood contract
a first-desi-on-MTV appearance
Please send me a talent
a cause for the interview
a ballgown to show off my . . . poise
Please send me a magazine
with my body in it
Please send me to Paradise
where I will wear the diamond tiara
& hula with Bob Barker
or Amitabh Bachchan
Please send me a rich
anesthesiologist
& a camel
& a needle's eye
to see him by
Please send me to the Festival of India parade
where I will float above
the huddled masses of my people
protesters from Khalistan
beaten wives   straight-A girls
immigrants with grease in their hair
hiphop boys with baggy pants & worried mothers
young white spouses slurping earnest curries
dealmakers   whiskeydrinkers
vegetarians eating just one chicken samosa
because it is our day
& this is our country
& I am so beautiful
& everything they imagined when they came
is true for at least one
24 karat gold afternoon.

Generica	America
In the land of the free	In the land of the free
we are eating french fries	we are eating kumquats
forty-seven percent	kohlrabi
of our daily vegetable intake:	
french fries	nopales
curly fries	
spicy fries	steamed bok choy on white rice
home fries	
Mickey D fries	portabello risotto
beer fries	
steak fries	tandoori pizza
chili fries	
fried fries	walrus pears
chicken-fried fries	
all fries gimme fries anykinda fries	shenandoah grapes
	okra
Touch us	We are rough-
we are always soft & smiling	edged
waxed lasered epilady'd	w/belly hairs
our skin smooth	& volatile
as the coating on Prozac	systems of belief
Gap-hued	turquoise of Guatemala cemeteries
we wear millennium blue	tangerine of Vietnam skies
	morning black
Still	
past Star Trek	
& Victoria's Secrets	
deep within	
the seventh circle of our souls	

individual as angels
or nightmares

our own fantasies
pulse

there where we have buried them   alive

CHITRA BANERJEE DIVAKARUNI

Born in India, Chitra Banerjee Divakaruni came to the United States in 1976. Her collections of poetry include *Leaving Yuba City* (Anchor Books, 1997), *Black Candle* (CALYX Press, 1991), and *The Reason for Nasturtiums* (The Berkeley Poets Workshop and Press, 1990). She has received both the Allen Ginsberg Prize and the Pushcart Prize for her poetry. Divakaruni has also published several novels, including *Palace of Illusions* (Doubleday, 2009), *Sister of My Heart* (Anchor, 2000) and *The Mistress of Spices* (Anchor, 1998). Her books for children include *Shadowland* (Roaring Brook Press, 2009) and *The Conch Bearer* (Aladdin, 2005). Divakaruni's collection of short stories, *Arranged Marriage* (Anchor, 1996), won the American Book Award. Her work has appeared in the *Atlantic Monthly,* the *New Yorker, Best American Short Stories,* and the Pushcart Prize anthology. She currently teaches creative writing at the University of Houston, Texas.

> *I think of myself as Bengali (through birth), Telugu (through marriage), and Indian American (through life choices).*

Yuba City School

From the black trunk I shake out
my one American skirt, blue serge
that smells of mothballs. Again today
Jagjit came crying from school. All week
the teacher has made him sit
in the last row, next to the boy
who drools and mumbles,
picks at the spotted milk-blue skin
of his face, but knows to pinch, sudden-sharp,
when she is not looking.

The books are full of black curves,
dots like the eggs the boll-weevil lays

each monsoon in furniture-cracks
in Ludhiana. Far up in front the teacher makes word-sounds
Jagjit does not know. They float
from her mouth-cave, he says,
in discs, each a different color.

Candy-pink for the girls in their lace dresses,
matching shiny shoes. Silk-yellow for the boys beside
them,
crisp blond hair, hands raised
in all the right answers. Behind them
the Mexicans, whose older brothers,
he tells me, carry knives,
whose catcalls and whizzing rubber bands clash, mid-air,
with the teacher's voice,
its sharp purple edge.

For him, the words are muddy red,
flying low and heavy,
and always the one he has learned to understand:
idiot idiot idiot.

I heat the iron over the stove. Outside
evening blurs the shivering
in the eucalyptus. Jagjit's shadow
disappears into the hole he is hollowing
all afternoon. The earth, he knows, is round,
and if he can tunnel all the way through,
he will end up in Punjab,
in his grandfather's mango orchard, his grandmother's songs
lighting on his head, the old words glowing
like summer fireflies.

In the playground, Jagjit says, invisible hands
snatch at his turban, expose
his uncut hair, unseen feet trip him from behind,

and when he turns, ghost laughter
all around his bleeding knees.
He bites down on his lip to keep in
the crying. They are
waiting for him to open his mouth,
so they can steal his voice.

I test the iron with little drops of water
that sizzle and die. Press down
on the wrinkled cloth. The room fills
with the smell like singed flesh.
Tomorrow in my blue skirt I will go
to see the teacher, my tongue
a stiff embarrassment in my mouth,
my few English phrases. She will pluck them from me,
nail shut my lips. My son will keep sitting
in the last row
among the red words that drink his voice.

The Geography Lesson

Look, says Sister Seraphina, *here is
the earth.* And holds up, by its base, the metal globe
dented from that time when Ratna, not looking,
knocked it off its stand and was sent
to Mother Superior. *And here
the axis on which it revolves, tilted
around the sun. Like this,* the globe a blur now,
land and water sloshed
into one muddy grey with the thick jab
of her finger.

Ratna returned to class with weal-streaked
palms, the left one bleeding slightly. She held it curled
in her lap so it wouldn't

stain her uniform as she wrote out,
one hundred times, *I will not damage*
school property again.

Now each girl sits with her silent laced shoes
flat on the classroom floor. I grip
my chair-edge. I know, were it not for the Grace
of the Holy Ghost, we would all
be swept off this madly spinning world
into perdition. Sometimes I feel it
at morning mass, six a.m. and the ground
under my knees sliding away, hot press
of air on the eardrum and the blue sleeves
of the Virgin opening
into tunnels.

Ratna didn't cry, so Sister Seraphina
pinned to her chest a placard that said,
in large black letters, WICKED. She
was to wear it till she repented, and no one
could speak to her.

This is the way the moon
travels around the earth, Sister
says, her fist circling the globe, solid,
tight-knuckled, pink nails
clipped back to the skin. I know
the moon, dense stone
suspended in the sky's chest,
which makes flood and madness happen and has
no light of its own. As our heathen souls
unless redeemed by Christ's blood.
That night in the moon-flecked dormitory
we woke to Ratna thrashing around in bed,
calling for Sultan, her dog back home. She
would not quiet when told,

and when the night nun tried
to give her water, she knocked the glass
away with a swollen hand. All
over the floor, shards, glittering
like broken eyes, and against the bed-rail
the flailing sound of her bones. Until they took her
somewhere downstairs.

On this chart, points Sister, *you see*
the major planets of the Solar System.
Copy them carefully into your notebooks. Smudges,
and you'll do them over. I outline
red Mars, ringed Saturn, the far cold gleam
of Uranus, their perfect, captive turning
around the black center which flames out
like the face of God in dreams. I will my hand
not to shake. We never saw Ratna again, and knew
not to ask.
Tomorrow we will be tested
on the various properties of the heavenly bodies,
their distance, in light years, from the sun.

Two Women Outside a Circus, Pushkar

after a photograph by Raghubir Singh

Faces pressed to the green stakes
of the circus fence, two village women,
red-veiled, with babies,
crouch low in the cloudy evening
breathing in the odors of the strange beasts
painted on the canvas above:
great black snakes with ruby eyes,
tigers with stars sewn onto their skins.
Beyond, a tent translucent with sudden light,

bits of exotic sound: gunshots, a growl,
a woman's raucous laugh.

The Nepal Circus demands
five rupees for entry to its neon world
of bears that dance, and porcupines
with arm-long poison quills. But five rupees
is a sack of *bajra* from Ramdin's store,
a week's dinner for the family. So the women
look and look
at the lighted sign of the lady acrobat.

In a short pink sequined skirt
she walks a tightrope
over gaping crocodile-jaws, twirling
her pink umbrella. Inside the tent,
the crowd shrieks as Master Pinto the Boy Wonder
is hurled from a flaming cannon. The women
clutch each other and search the sky
for the thunder-sound. Ecstatic applause.
The band plays a hit from *Mera Naam Joker*
and the crowd sings along.

The women gather their babies
and head home to the canvas of their lives:
endless coarse *rotis*
rolled in smoky kitchens, slaps or caresses
from husbands with palm-wine breaths, whining,
clutching children and more in the belly, perhaps
a new green skirt at harvest time.

But each woman
tending through burning noon the blinkered bull
that circles, all day, the *bajra*-crushing stones,
or wiping in dark the sweat
of unwanted sex from her body, remembers

in sparkling tights the woman acrobat
riding a one-wheeled cycle so immense
her head touches the stars. Remembers
the animal trainer in her leopard skins,
holding a blazing hoop through which leap
endless smiling lions.

Indian Movie, New Jersey

Not like the white filmstars, all rib
and gaunt cheekbone, the Indian sex-goddess
smiles plumply from behind a flowery
branch. Below her brief red skirt, her thighs
are satisfying-solid, redeeming
as tree trunks. She swings her hips
and the men-viewers whistle. The lover-hero
dances in to a song, his lip-sync
a little off, but no matter, we
know the words already and sing along.
It is safe here, the day
golden and cool so no one sweats,
roses on every bush and the Dal Lake
clean again.
The sex goddess switches
to thickened English to emphasize
a joke. We laugh and clap. Here
we need not be embarrassed by words
dropping like lead pellets into foreign ears.
The flickering movie-light
wipes from our faces years of America, sons
who want mohawks and refuse to run
the family store, daughters who date on the sly.
When at the end the hero
dies for his friend who also
loves the sex-goddess and now can marry her,
we weep, understanding. Even the men

clear their throats to say, "What *qurbani!*
What *dosti!*" After, we mill around
unwilling to leave, exchange greetings
and good news: a new gold chain, a trip
to India. We do not speak
of motel raids, canceled permits, stones
thrown through glass windows, daughters and sons
raped by Dotbusters.
In this dim foyer
we can pull around us the faint, comforting smell
of incense and *pakoras,* can arrange
our children's marriages with hometown boys and girls,
open a franchise, win a million
in the mail. We can retire
in India, a yellow two-storied house
with wrought-iron gates, our own
Ambassador car. Or at least
move to a rich white suburb, Summerfield
or Fort Lee, with neighbors that will
talk to us. Here while the film-songs still echo
in the corridors and restrooms, we can trust
in movie truths: sacrifice, success, love and luck,
the America that was supposed to be.

SEJAL SHAH

Born and raised in Rochester, New York, Sejal Shah received an under-graduate degree in English from Wellesley College (where she was awarded the Academy of American Poets Prize) and an MFA (fiction) from the University of Massachusetts at Amherst. Her writing has appeared in the *Asian Pacific American Journal, Catamaran,* the *Indiana Review,* the *Massachusetts Review, Meridians, Pleiades, Prairie Fire,* and the anthologies *Under Her Skin* (Seal Press, 2004) and *Contours of the Heart: South Asians Map North America* (Asian American Writers' Workshop, 1996). Shah has been awarded residencies by the Blue Mountain Center, the New York State Council for the Arts, and the Millay Colony. Her poem "Independence, Iowa" was performed in an evening-length dance piece, "Ball's Out: Play to Win," presented by the Black Earth Collaborative Arts Company (Iowa). She is an assistant professor of English at Marymount Manhattan College.

> *Though the daughter of Gujarati parents from Ahmedabad and Nairobi, I have been to India twice and Kenya never.*

Everybody's Greatest Hits

We were dancing to Marvin Gaye in my living room. That's how you said you knew where you would sleep. We were dancing to CDs you bought in Thailand. Of course they were boot-legged. Every name was misspelled.

Let's go somewhere together! We'll hand each other black sweaters and malaria pills. We'll go away. A small wedding, a large country, a long walk. South, for loose shirts, custom-sewn for pennies. North, to practice a language you haven't used in years. Every word when leaving has direction. Every word when leaving is about pointing. Pointing is always about leaving. Lying is only leaving before you go.

Take our daughter. I'd tell her things. Daughter, I'd say, you don't have to have wood floors. Don't listen to those others. If fifty-fifty is good enough

for your mother, it's good enough for you. Don't wash your hair every day.
Americans are wasteful like that. Who else has that kind of water?

Watch the blue circle hovering behind each thing a person ever says.
It's the truth-teller. Solder your sentences with unnecessary light:
diaphanous, solipsism, hegemony, cataract.

Let's elide the things we won't talk about.
Let's accumulate like horses in the darker corners.

Accordion

You are insufficiently Jewish.
I am hesitation.

You are two bridges, a rush of light.
You will see only the girders, remember only the glint.

I'm ready to give up on silver rings and recycling.
I'm ready for a name change, jealousy, drives to Vermont.

Here is my works cited.
Here is my interview with the Lord.
I have no sources. I can't remember how to parachute.

Your words all seem brighter than mine. For example:

"He seemed a very pleasant young man," you replied,
drying dishes all the while—and
"I looked in on you while you were gone."

You told me I look different in glasses. Everyone does.
I was worried. I reached for lipstick.
You said I seemed so much younger. Doesn't everyone?

What I wanted was protection, was to see. To lean against
the bar, half-lit, and look into the half-lit places. To unfurl.

What does it matter if your hands are gone from me?
This apostrophic vein wears me. You carotid me.
These obdurate persimmons stack themselves around me.

Independence, Iowa

In Decorah, the train station became a chiropractor's office
(Everything was once something else—)

We are driving up along the Mississippi because I did not push
to look at the map myself and you wanted to get lost. I mean:
now we are watching a train go by, blocks of red—
and driving on a blue bridge while the light is bright that way it is
before falling. The only choices are Wisconsin or Illinois:
to take 52 up through Dubuque, or to stop. To rest.

It's the sound of the wheels on the bridge
hollow, before I finally have a moment, of lift.

Driving back from Cedar Rapids, we pass cornfields: stalks dying,
stalks dried. Independence has the most beautiful train station—
I think the country out here is full of them. We passed a train when driving.
You said: I'd like to hop trains some day. The world is full of things
we haven't done. Or said. In this corner of Iowa I feel far from every place else.
The most beautiful train station was once something else.

We stopped in a town you had once visited with someone else. I wanted to
    take you
to a restaurant that I love. One that reminds me of another place I once
    lived: the wooden bar
jewel-like lighting along tracks. Each bridge is that bridge, each smattering
    of lights, those lights
I remember, all the ways in which they sang out. It was Christmas every
    night in Brooklyn.

Just walking was a view. I live here now, that place Easterners insist is big
  sky, paper-flat.

But the sky was more than big. It was everything. And so much of our drive
was through land that curved; that was not, and never had been, flat.

NEELANJANA BANERJEE

Neelanjana Banerjee's poetry and fiction have appeared in the *Literary Review*, the *Asian Pacific American Journal*, *Nimrod*, *A Room of One's Own*, *Desilit*, and the anthology *Desilicious* (Arsenal Pulp Press, 2004). She received an MFA in creative writing from San Francisco State University in 2007 and was a Hedgebrook fellow in 2008. Banerjee has worked in mainstream, ethnic, and independent media for the past ten years. She edits the Books and Literature section for *Hyphen* (an Asian American magazine based in the San Francisco Bay Area). She has helped young people tell their own stories at YO! Youth Outlook Multimedia and as a teaching artist with WritersCorps. Banerjee lives in San Francisco and is currently working on a collection of short stories.

> I am a Midwestern-born, West Coast–transplanted, Bengali-speaking, South Asian American, person of color, Asian American feminist writer.

Cowgirl Series, I

Radha Meets Calamity Jane
There was a bout of smallpox
once in Vrindavan too,

Radha says, fingering a
nearly heart-shaped cowpox
scar under her thumb.

Jane sighs, spits a wad of chew
and says: "Surviving is harder than
living."

Calamity Jane Says to Radha

If he were mine, I'd have strung him
up like a rabbit, I'd have cut him with a meat
cleaver like I done to Jack McCall after he shot
Wild Bill in the back of the head, I'd leave him
in Sioux County without a horse or a weapon—
them people got their own gods, they won't
give a hoot about his blue ass.

A Quiet Moment w/ Calamity Jane and Radha

Chapatis make a flap flapping
sound against Radha's palms, her
bangles tinkle like cowbells.

Jane sets her boots heavily on
the porch railing, swills her whiskey
in a glass.

They are both thinking of the way the light
looks in the dust the cows kick up at the end of the day.

Priapos

At Ephesus, the tour guide wipes his forehead,
tells us about Priapos, son of Aphrodite. Born
cursed: huge belly, hands, nose, tongue and a gigantic,
continuously erect phallus. Sunburned white men
snicker, pose their wives next to the squat stone figure.

You pull me behind a row of pillars, put your hand
under my skirt. I listen to the tour guide: Due to his
ugliness, Priapos was abandoned in the wilderness
where his presence made plants shoot up from the earth,
animals copulate furiously. Sweat drips off the tip of your nose.

That night at the bar, you get too drunk with your
brother, talk loudly about what it was like to get
your cock pierced, shatter a glass. They say Priapos was more
than his anatomy: he taught grace to Ares. Teaching
the young god to dance before he knew anything of war.

On the way back to the hotel, I balance your stumbles, soothe
your slurs. In bed, you mumble and bite hieroglyphics
into my breasts, then pass out. It was women who prayed to
Priapos: placing his effigy in corners to ward off the evil
eye, burying him deep under their marital bed
to bless their men with his misfortune.

AMARNATH RAVVA

Amarnath Ravva received an MFA in writing and integrated media from the California Institute of the Arts and a BA in comparative literature from the University of California, Berkeley. He has performed (as part of the ambient improvisational ensemble Ambient Force 3000) at the Los Angeles County Museum of Art, Machine Project, and Betalevel. He has also exhibited work at Telic, the Acorn Gallery, Pond, and the Keith and Janet Kellogg University Art Gallery. His work has appeared in journals such as *nocturnes (re)view of the literary arts, Encyclopedia* (vol. 2), *LA-Lit,* and *Drunken Boat.*

I am a Telugu Californian who was born in upstate New York and lived in Hyderabad, Andhra Pradesh, as a young child.

I Am Burning a Pig in My Room, Apollinaire

You speak of
the heavenly bee
Arcture, resting fat
in bed with gauze
above your brows
that covers
the contingent wound
from the war

you received the
shell that
split your
head
while reading

    before meeting
you I was
    young with my father

on a country ranch
on a swing   they were
hunting the pig
for lunch, heard
horny rusted snorts
cornered across
the field

the spit turned
above the cedar fire
when he pointed, not
at my falling
shin but the bee
I swung into, who
killed himself
and clung
still
in my shin

        later,
the pig died
roasting
it was
heavenly
like you are
when read

but you're
the stiff in the photo
I meet daily, the reading
and shelving of
what's left
of you
gets to
my baby head

you did not ask
to die
of the wound
and the Spanish
Grippe that
seized you
soon after,
laying you
prostrate in bed
for a still
life

the Grippe
ran through
you, burning and
boiling your water
out past the skin
gripping and tossing
your gauze ridden
body in the
waiting grass

    now night
comes and
hours ring
where accidents
have left you
sheaved, in
my hands.

Bear Scat Flat

I never knew I'd come
to Bear Scat Flat
but there it was
around cabins with walls

as thin
as a toy house
teeming with life, mosquitoes
borrowing your own
for the night

and in their drone
the miner's dead horse-
dredger, crusher, ore skip
rusts light
on the ground

there are machines in the forest
and a bear on the floor
and my hand
slips
and snaps
my face

we move faster to catch up with
what's endless around us
stars, like the buzz, burning
on my neck

and sipping beer
till Liz picks it up
and says,
this is where
the bullet
went in

the bear:

     hung like a dog
by hands she cleaned
my furry wound with,

"I am the mouth
she ate with flesh
years ago, I am
the young
throat
she swallows"

When I was young trains cast light
across the straits as they passed
the kids of Port Costa
looking back
at the lights
of Benicia

like now when
I look at Liz
over the table the bear the rug
between us,
                    it's
not the first time I've
seen a dead bear
the last was
                    draped over
the body of a man who sweat
animation

into the bear tied

to his back

as he danced

as we watched

his eyes

showing white

showing red

veins crossing

as he snorts
in the circle

we made
in dance
for him

whose heart
beat fast
as we turned,

blue mayflies in June brushing
him

with wormwood.

the spectacle of a few trees in spring, off the 5.

I.

The birds travel miles
to mate here with us
at the rest stop, changing
the trees into a carnal city
they drop adulterous waters
from, bathe the bobbing
lufkins in the fields
with their homage

It's spring and they feel
oil underground like
heat that turns
them on
                        they should
look at the sign
stuck in the lawn
facing the dry hills to the south
like the ones around a lake
near my childhood home,
                        it says there
are rattlesnakes in the area
active at night in the summer
when I was younger, before the hills
were covered with streets
and cul-de-sacs named
after flowers, I'd make out
with a girl thinking
of sex and dry ground, of
rattlesnakes and refineries
staining the sky with
compulsion like the birds
above me now,
drawn to the spectacle of a few trees
in spring.

                        II.

When I was older I met you,
and you painted faces
contorted by years
of living in L.A.

Back then we learned the city
by having sex in the car, watched

the tar covered mastodon
stand still in its pit

At night we went to clubs
in Hollywood, were
spectators to acts
on stage in throbbing
light
                    as they would
bring out a naked man
chained like a dog,
and sodomize him while he ate Alpo.

III.

Three years later you show me a woman you drew
from chalk with eyes more living
than your own, a sparkle
on the dead wall you chose
as canvas, and with you
is your friend you call
"The Art Nun" because she is
celibate, fifty, and grew up
in this city where sex
is like cars,
and swallowed
like water.

MYTILI JAGANNATHAN

Mytili Jagannathan is the author of *Acts*, a chapbook from Habenicht Press, and her poems have appeared in *Rattapallax, Sous Rature, Mirage#4/ Period[ical], Combo, Fanzine, Interlope, Xcp: Cross-Cultural Poetics,* and the "Queering Language" issue of *EOAGH*. Her poetry is also part of a recent collaboration with the filmmaker Sara Zia Ebrahimi for the Termite TV Collective. Jagannathan's awards include an Inspiration Grant from the Leeway Foundation and a Pew Fellowship in the Arts. Jagannathan earned a BA from Brandeis University and an MA from the University of Pennsylvania; she also studied for a year in Madurai, India. Jagannathan lives in Philadelphia, where she teaches at the Community College of Philadelphia and runs her own consulting business, Itinerant Ink.

Iowa-born and West Virginia–raised, I speak Niligiri-and-Kerala-inflected Tamil—which made me instantly identifiable in Madurai.

nationalism redactor

when agitation and
remorse are present in us
who is aware?
agitation and remorse
present us to ourselves   but only
sometimes sentient. when they are
absent   in what fields do they
hide Monsanto green?
when agitation and remorse
begin to arise are you
wearing the right
armor? in Ayodhya: Brindavan:
does it rain   redress
explain   Bombay?
or soldier flare fulfill

the Vedas and Pokhran
will they pay you
in coin or in salve?
the sign dissolves the
camera solves resisting
bodies India day parade.

when already arisen
agitation and remorse
are abandoned   the country
slips into the disputed river.
saffron clash   supplied
defiance   depends on women
lining up for water.
clamor: breathe: it's august
nineteen ninety eight the desert
holds. suffer in
what attribute
whose skin?
worship did not
divide us but now
the lord and headlines tell us
so. becomes a fact,
accomplished.
                            fold over fold over

                    already abandoned
agitation and remorse. who   is aware.
torn cloth of subsistence, a flag, agitation.
mercy.   will not arise,
the future. already,
remorse. already
abandoned.

Dream House

or it was in the chosen
stark supplanted dark

that I encountered
sequence of roofs, rain

sliding off—terraced
cyclamens—and deep

in the forest of values
I dissembled a gun

duration endured
intercepted plunder—

collusion of foliage
density squared and hot

chlorophyll poured
down storm's

garment and
body overtook me

SRIKANTH REDDY

Srikanth Reddy's first collection of poetry, *Facts for Visitors* (University of California Press, 2004), received the 2005 Asian American Literary Award for Poetry. His poems have also appeared in *American Poetry Review, Grand Street, Fence,* and *Ploughshares,* and his critical writing has been featured in publications such as the *New Republic,* the *Chicago Tribune,* and *American Literature.* He has held fellowships from the Mellon Foundation, the Whiting Foundation (in the Humanities), and the Wisconsin Institute for Creative Writing. A graduate of the Iowa Writers' Workshop and the doctoral program in English at Harvard University, Reddy is currently an assistant professor of English at the University of Chicago.

I was born in Chicago to Telugu parents from Andhra Pradesh.

Jungle Book

Once as we scavenged in the jungle I asked my friend
about sadness. "How will I know when it comes?"
He was up on his haunches, pulling at a leafy branch

I couldn't reach. "First learn about jackfruit," he said,
handing me a ripe one. It smelled heavy & delicate,
like my friend. "Break it. What do you see?"

"Only these seeds," I said, "& all exceedingly small."
My friend scratched where the trap bit into him years ago,
& a steady stream of green ants carried a moth wing

across the footpath. It passed like a sail or a fin.
"Break one," he said. "Now what do you see?"
I split open a seed with the edge of my thumbnail

& cupped it in the palms of my hands & squinted
under the smoky light coming down slantwise
through the treetops. There was a glistening new plant

folded up inside, with one grey leaf on a dark stem
the length of an eyelash. It sprang to life
& put out hundreds of jackfruit blossoms all at once

but when I said your name they blew everywhere.

Scarecrow Eclogue

Then I took the poem in my hand & walked out
past the well & three leveled acres
to where the sugarcane built itself slowly to the songs of young goats
& there at the field's shimmering center

I inserted the page
into the delicately-woven grass of the scarecrow's upraised hand
where it began to shine & give a little in the gentle
unremitting breeze sent over from the east.

I stepped back several paces
to look at what I'd done.
Only a little way off & the morning light bleached out my ink
on the page so it simplified

into a white rectangle against a skyblue field
flapping once, twice
as if grazed by one close shot after another.
The oxen snorted nearby

& there was a sense of publication
but not much else was different, so I backed off all the way
to the sugarcane's edge until the poem was only a gleam
among the fieldworkers' sickles surfacing

like the silver backs of dolphins
up above the green crop-rows into view, then down from view.
How it shone in my withdrawal,
worksongs rising

over it all. So then I said the poem aloud, my version
of what the god dressed up as a charioteer said
to the reluctant bowman
at the center of the battlefield.

How he spoke of duty, the substance
of this world,
& the trembling armies ranged.

Fundamentals of Esperanto

The grammatical rules of this language can be learned in one
sitting.

Nouns have no gender & end in -o; the plural terminates in -oj
(pronounced -oy) & the accusative, -on (plural -ojn).

Amiko, friend; amikoj, friends; amikon & amikojn, accusative
friend & friends.

Adjectives end in –a & take plural & accusative endings to
agree with things.

Ma amiko is my friend.

All verbs are regular & have only one form for each tense or
mood; they are not altered for person or number. Mi havas
bonajn amikojn is simply to say I have good friends.

Adverbs end in –e.

La bonaj amiko estas ie. The good friend is here.

-

A new book appears in Esperanto every week. Radio stations in
Europe, the United States, China, Russia & Brazil broadcast in
Esperanto, as does Vatican Radio. In 1959, UNESCO declared the
International Federation of Esperanto Speakers to be in accord with
its mission & granted this body consultative status. The youth
branch of the International Federation of Esperanto Speakers, UTA,
has offices in 80 different countries & organizes social events where
young people curious about the movement may dance to recordings
by Esperanto artists, enjoy complimentary soft drinks & take home
Esperanto versions of major literary works including the Old
Testament & *A Midsummer Night's Dream.* William Shatner's first
feature-length vehicle was a horror film shot entirely in Esperanto.
Esperanto is among the languages currently sailing into deep space
on board the Voyager spacecraft.

-

Esperanto is an artificial language
constructed in 1887 by L.
   L. Zamenhof, a polish
      oculist. I first came
across *Fundamento Esperanto,* the text
   which introduced this system
      to the world, as I traveled abroad

following a somewhat difficult period
in my life. It was twilight & snowing on the
   railway platform just outside
      Warsaw where I had missed
my connection. A man in a crumpled track suit
   & dark glasses pushed a cart
      piled high with ripped & weathered volumes—

sex manuals, detective stories, yellowing
musical scores & outdated physics textbooks,
 old copies of *Life,* new smut,
  an atlas translated,
a grammar, *The Mirror,* Soviet-bloc comics,
 a guide to the rivers &
  mountains, thesauri, inscrutable

musical scores & mimeographed physics books,
defective stories, obsolete sex manuals—
  one of which caught my notice
  (Dr. Esperanto,
Zamenhof's pen name, translates as He Who Hopes) &
 since I had time, I traded
  my used *Leaves of Grass* for a copy.

-

Mi amas vin, bela amiko.
I'm afraid I will never be lonely enough.
There's a man from Quebec in my head,

a friend to the purple martins.
Purple martins are the Cadillac of swallows.
All purple martins are dying or dead.
Brainscans of grown purple martins suggest
these creatures feel the same levels of doubt

& bliss as an eight-year-old girl in captivity.
While driving home from the brewery
one night this man from Quebec heard a radio program
about purple martins & the next day he set out
to build them a house
in his own back yard. I've never built anything,
let alone a house,

not to mention a home
for somebody else.

I've never unrolled a blueprint onto a workbench,
sunk a post,
or sent the neighbor's kid pedalling off
to the store for a bag full of nails.

I've never waited ten years for a swallow.

Never put in aluminum floors to smooth over the waiting.
Never piped sugar water through colored tubes
to each empty nest lined with newspaper shredded
with strong, tired hands.
Never dismantled the entire affair

& put it back together again.
Still no swallows.
I never installed the big light that stays on through the night

to keep owls away. Never installed lesser lights,
never rested on Sunday

with a beer on the deck surveying
what I had done
& what yet remained to be done, listening to Styx

while the neighbor kids ran through my sprinklers.
I have never collapsed in abandon.
Never prayed.
But enough about purple martins.

-

As we speak, Esperanto is being corrupted
by upstart languages such as Interlingua,
Klingon, Java & various cryptophasic tongues.

Our only hope of reversing this trend is to write
the Esperanto epic. Through its grandeur
& homegrown humility, it will spur men

to freeze the mutating patois so the children
of our children's children may dwell in this song
& find comfort in its true texture & frame.

It's worth a try. As I imagine it, it ends
in the middle of things. Every line of the work
is a first & a last line & this is the spring

of its action. Of course, there's a journey
& inside that journey, an implicit voyage
through the underworld. There's a bridge

made of boats; a carp stuffed with flowers;
a comic dispute among sweetmeat vendors;
a digression on shadows; men clapping

in fields to scare away crows; an unending list
of warships: *The Unternehmen, The Impresa,*
The Muyarchi, Viec Lam, The Przedsiebiorstwo,

The Indarka, The Enterprise, L'Entreprise,
Entrepeno . . . One could go on. But by now,
all the characters have turned into swallows

& bank as one flock in the sky—that is,
all except one. That's how we finally learn
who the hero was all along. Weary & old,

he sits on a rock & watches his friends
fly one by one out of the song,
then turns back to the journey they all began

long ago, keeping the river to his right.

Corruption

I am about to recite a psalm that I know. Before I begin, my expectation extends over the entire psalm. Once I have begun, the words I have said remove themselves from expectation & are now held in memory while those yet to be said remain waiting in expectation. The present is a word for only those words which I am now saying. As I speak, the present moves across the length of the psalm, which I mark for you with my finger in the psalm book. The psalm is written in India ink, the oldest ink known to mankind. Every ink is made up of a color & a vehicle. With India ink, the color is carbon & the vehicle, water. Life on our planet is also composed of carbon & water. In the history of ink, which is rapidly coming to an end, the ancient world turns from the use of India ink to adopt sepia. Sepia is made from octopus, the squid & the cuttlefish. One curious property of the cuttlefish is that, once dead, its body begins to glow. This mild phosphorescence reaches its greatest intensity a few days after death, then ebbs away as the body decays. You can read by this light.

PRAGEETA SHARMA

The first of her family born outside of India, Massachusetts-born Prageeta Sharma is the author of three poetry collections: *Infamous Landscapes* (Fence Books, 2007), *The Opening Question* (Fence Books, 2004), and *Bliss to Fill* (Subpress, 2000). *The Opening Question* won the 2004 Modern Poets Prize. Her work has appeared in journals such as *Agni,* the *Boston Review,* the *Indiana Review, jubilat,* and the *Literary Review.* Sharma is an associate professor of English (poetry) and the director of the Creative Writing Program at the University of Montana in Missoula. Her current projects include her next poetry collection (working title *Undergloom*), a novel (*Halogen*), and an artist's book created in collaboration with the artist Hedya Klein. Sharma lives in Montana and Seattle with her husband, the composer Dale Edwin Sherrard.

> *I am of Rajasthani heritage but was born in Massachusetts. I arrived a few years after my father had his first truly American experience: attending Woodstock.*

Paper

Her sunlit rooms defend a dark complexion,
a succeeding doom, a mausoleum.
The day when gift-giving achieves only serious pangs of loneliness.
She could not recall anyone's earnest gestures.
The terrible light needs graceful navigators.
The crossroads near the parkways are too far
for her to gather rooms to take back to her things.

On one occasion she watched a small boy on the corner of Freemont and Ives
drag a toy truck against the sidewalk
and it was the same effect of tracing a single finger along a ream of paper.

This was how she found the unannounced guest,
writing with her pen at her desk,
no real obliterations to her yard, this she found was not carelessness.

Paper II

There had been enough time for her to become an adult
without it having too much of an effect on her parents'

nervous system. She had certainly told them in a slow,
honest way, with a pre-planned epiphany—that she had lovers.

Madhu and Raju, her parents, out of their arranged marriage
grew a rhyme. And their daughter grew into a poet.

Or she grew into a lover which was taking up all her time
and poetry was only a series of mistakes worth claiming

to a page and not a lover.

I Cannot Forget You

There are populated gestures
in the dining room where we become public
partners of a compromise. If I never lift this explosive

to show the little complexity of diction,
I shall never feel certain if I have lived
a satisfying life. I am unsure of the urgency

that lies beneath shyness. Compelled to negotiate,
I speak out of turn. There is nothing
one can do when they behave poorly.

In Open Water, In Mathematical Star

After Breton

The glove was lost under the twinkling of night, under the premise
of an open pocket, and led me to the question of captivity with a brass

timepiece calculating the motion, it was in the midst of a blush.
In the desire for suspension, for speed, you beamed, and this led

mathematically to the pupil of evening, the gossamer cast
overlooking noon and of the formula of morning loose over the hands

while it was your vodka that was clear. All who had been driving
pulled over to touch weather in rare bodily grain.

SASHA KAMINI PARMASAD

Sasha Kamini Parmasad was born in Trinidad and raised in both Trinidad and New Delhi, India. As a child, she was actively involved in the performing arts (poetry, calypso, story-telling, and Indian Trinidadian folk songs) at a national level in Trinidad and Tobago. In the late 1990s, Parmasad moved to the United States, where she received her undergraduate degree from Williams College, followed by an MFA in creative writing from Columbia University in 2008. She is currently an essayist, video artist, and painter in New York City, where she teaches creative writing. Her poem "Memory of Sugarcane-worker Off Duty" won the 2008 Poetry International competition, while her first novel, *Ink and Sugar,* placed third in the national First Words Literary Contest for South Asian Writers in 2003. Her art has been exhibited at the Commonwealth Institute (UK) and MASS MoCA.

> *A South Asian in New York, I am also a sixth-generation Trinidadian,*
> *descendant of jahajees; I think of the Caribbean as my blood, India,*
> *my inherited bones.*

Burning

for Soobratan

The twelve o'clock sun sizzles
like onions and garlic the grandmother pitches
into a black iron pot rubbed with butter.
Trees are stingy with their shade.
Moth-winged morning flowers wither on stems.

The girl stands before a dusty window
blinking sweat from eyes, scraping
muck from neck.

A squealing hog gallops into their road
roiling
begging for mercy it does not receive
from her father who, cooing
like a dove, plunges
a knife into its back.
Throws a wire noose about its neck.
Drags it writhing
back to the slaughtery.—
Pig's blood staining the macadam road forever.

The onions burn like skin
but the grandmother continues to stir, slowly
sing a song;
then thick shriek of a hog
and silence,
far as the church spire.

Gnawing lips
the girl unlatches the kitchen door,
walks outside, barefoot,
sniffs air before stooping
in bleeding gravel
to observe lines of ants
marching oblivious,
and whisper,
Fetch me a hose.

Sugarcane Farmer

for Selina

We visit her after thirty odd years
winding down
ribbon road straddling

sugar plains;
bitches in heat beneath milky ocean
of ripe cane-arrows.

Barrackpur cantonment, India, 1857—
Cartridge cases greased
with beef and pig fat
the last straw, sparking
revolt.
Barrackpore, Trinidad, 1975—
Place of her parents, grandparents, five generations
talvar-bearing sepoy folded
into her, and she leaping
cutlass in hand, onto bison cart,
seizing reins, charging past
brandished police butus
to occupy No. 4 Scale, Valley Line,
push gun barrel from her face,
barefoot, anger thick-bitter
rusted, invisible hunger-chains strapped
to her ankles—
Ashes in the water
Ashes in the sea
We all rise up
With a one, two, three!

Afterwards the consequences:
her cane refused
by the Company for two years.
Rotting, stinking sugar-stalks.
Nothing
like that smell.
"Give me a drake, come clean
my front step," a big farmer said.
His yard was dark, reeking of drakes.
She scrubbed, he bought
her dying cane.

"We heard you were dead."
"No, sixty-six years and still struggling," she says,
shoulders torn
bosom pinned
mahogany feet too hard for shoes.
She coughs,
offers us coconuts from a tree.
Does not tell us, *No money*
for my operation or
to make groceries this week.
We cool our throats,
toss hard nuts into soft bush,
talk
about blood, her sepoy inheritance.
Laugh
make promises
depart.
"Not in vain!" she waves,
"We struggle hard together
in a loving, peaceful way."

We do not call her.
We forget.
She waits.
To dust, she waits.

The Old Man

He tells me
about Tamil Tigers.
Enough is enough, says he:
It go take just one crazy coolie to
strap bombs to his heart
walk into the middle of this Carnival-land
and mash it up forever.

One crazy, mad-ass coolie,
chest too full of clotted blood,
swollen like an over-ripe mango
ready to burst
ablaze with love for snake-infested rice fields
rotting mangrove swamps
sugarcane plains watered with
generations of sweat,
muddy rivers made holy
by ashes of the dead,
every ravine
tree
stone
bird
to let him stand, frigid
and hear them say again
in the noon hours of a second century:

Stay in your place, Mr. Coolie-man.
Go back where you come from;
Iere is not yours to love.

Enough is Enough, the old man says,
his face a ploughed ocean
where light can lose its way:
This knot of sinking land
so precious
as it is
to half a million of us coolies
with no other home.

Just one crazy coolie.

VIVEK JAIN

Vivek Jain was born in Bhopal, India, in 1980 and spent his boyhood in Appalachia. He earned an undergraduate degree in biochemistry from the University of Virginia. Currently, Jain is a resident physician with interests in psychiatry, psychoanalysis, and public health. He also enjoys the reimagined poetry of translation. Jain lives in Richmond, Virginia, with his younger brother, Anand, and their mother.

I find labels—whether imposed by an external world of which I have limited knowledge or adopted by an emerging sense of self— problematic. After all, isn't the project of self-knowledge a lifelong endeavor?

Poem for a Would-be Revolutionary, My Father

My father's beard winters.
      His sister intimates how,
years ago, Indira's men first sought
      him in the night, how
prison submerged his life.

Five times, papa, they came for you.

How their negotiations
      with wrist-thick bamboo sounded
like deference
      or a beaten pariah.
You descended each time,
      your protests preceded by conviction.

Anand's Story

god didn't make me—

At dusk, I escaped
from the foundry
of India.

Atop the pyre,
I seized the urgent
smoke roots
of the dark banyan cloud
over Bhopal.

From the altitude of god I fell,
depositing,
and pocked
the sphere below.

From there, I wandered
to play in the laps
of hills.

You, who have forgotten
how these eyes were once
backlit with death, know this:

god didn't make me,
I wasn't his to make.

December, 1984

The reports drift in.

Conjured from among twenty
thousand who swilled

mouthfuls, lungfuls,
vaporous biting dreams

that came foraging
mistaking it for the night dhool

is my brother, pushing
through growing mounds

of hardening limbs
as woodpiles' flames confuse brown

skin for bark. He is displaced
on the flocculent

ashes of twenty-thousand sleepers
broadening in the sky,

an estuary.
This December night sews lights

on shores where others join
stacks of blazes,

like wicks upon wicks,
in the city, Bhopal.

RO GUNETILLEKE

Sri Lankan–born Ro Gunetilleke writes in Hermosa Beach, California. His poems and short stories have appeared in *Catamaran, Muse India, Poetic Diversity,* and the *Best of the Net 2006* anthology (Sundress Publications, 2007). His work has been featured at Artwallah (2004 and 2005), Beyond Baroque's Spring 2005 poetry series, the New Short Fiction series at the Beverly Hills Public Library, and the Newer Poets reading, part of the Los Angeles Public Library's Aloud series. He recently completed his first novel, *Bad Karma Girl.*

> *I lived through the 1983 communal riots in Colombo Sri Lanka and shed my national identity. I see myself as a Sri Lanka-born Californian.*

Lost Column

For Richard de Souza

Bite marks on the wall,
boot stains on the rug,
your crumpled red tee shirt
chokes on the wrecked bed.

They sniffed around in your room for hours,
clawed through the shadows,
lifted prints off your thoughts,
left with your satchel, spilling words along the lawn.

No scrapbook of your columns,
no tin box of your poems,
no pirith chant,
no séance.

In the belly of the jungle,
on a pyre of tires,
they erased you
word by word.

Spirited Away

After the third dram,
he lifts the shot glass
to the gas lamp,
looking for that last
drop of coconut arrack,
the slurred words
come
looking for me.

Marconi shortwave radio
coughs to the crackle of
coconut-shell firepot,
grandpa's lap feels
like our satin couch,
I sink in.

Grandpa shuttles the radio dial,
I hold the hairpin antenna,
wiggle it just a hair
this way or that way,
and we are off,
across the world
in Greenwich meantime,
to a world that meant
nothing
but was everything.

Grandpa's thumb
nimble on the dial,

first stop Lucknow
then to Moscow,
Swan Lake he says,
sways his chin like a metronome.

We hear ten languages
in one night,
music and gibberish
like shadow puppets,
we make up names
for the song, the tune
that finds us,
we make it all our own.

It is 1956.
Fires burn
Jaffna to Colombo.

Mani's bakery charred,
no more honey-buns
with sprinkled sugar caps.
Mani went away
with the Red Cross,
fifteen years bundled in a gunnysack.

Grandpa shuts the window
downs the third dram,
kindles the firepot,
and sinks into the chair,
all arms and legs.

I bend the hairpin to the North
we run away again.

AMITAVA KUMAR

Amitava Kumar is the author of *Husband of a Fanatic* (The New Press, 2005), *Bombay-London-New York* (Routledge, 2002), and *Passport Photos* (University of California Press, 2000). His novel, *Home Products* (Picador India, 2007), was short-listed for India's premier literary prize, the Crossword Book Award. His latest book, A *Foreigner Carrying in the Crook of His Arm a Tiny Bomb,* is a writer's report on the global war on terror (Duke University Press, 2010). Kumar is a professor of English at Vassar College and lives in Poughkeepsie, New York.

> *I am a resident father, a non-resident Indian, and a global citizen of the world created by Bollywood.*

Mistaken Identity

For June Jordan

The dried black map of ink spilt on the blotting paper
spreads to the armpit of the policeman's uniform as he searches for the file
shoving aside the candle stub, the underwear with thick blue stripes,
the empty pint of Sailor's, stale newspapers and the film heroine's
sideways glance, with the year's calendar stamped beneath her bulging
    breasts, engaging Mahatma Gandhi's patriotic and virtuous toothless
    grin. The file,
once found, will allow the policeman to record a case of mistaken identity
when a poor farmer drank the lethal drops of the pesticide synthetic
    pyrethroid
he had earlier bartered his remaining water buffalo and his wife's jewels for
and months later the crops still failed because the chemical didn't slow down
the hardy sweet-potato whiteflies—though it did work on the farmer
and thirty-six other suicides in the village.

The world is cool and dim blue inside the tall newspaper building
where safe from the stutter and the smoke of auto-rickshas, buses filled
to impossibility, and the dust he hates as much he hates slogans, the editor
    turns
the stem of his pipe fragrant with the smell of Dutch tobacco away from the
    chaos outside to offer to the young reporters in his office metaphors of
    mistaken identity. When Rajiv Gandhi was killed you know that the
    Congress youth set fire to countless buses and public buildings in
    Madras, and even started riots in several other places,
but when you write about the others, the leftist activists who enraged by
    illegal police killings on any particular day decide to burn buses or police
    stations, and murder
a landlord who might or might not have raped and butchered a peasant on
    his land,
you have to hold accountable these leftists who, unlike the Congress youth, are
after all responsible for starting a vicious circle—by inviting the police
to go on a killing spree in revenge.

In a suburban, American home standing on a Kashmiri carpet
that has been brought from India the last time relatives came here to visit,
as you offer these riddles to flavor the dinner of tandoori and saffron-col-
    ored biryani,
your host sips his scotch which back home he would buy for nine hundred
    rupees
on the black market, and then he feels secure enough to say that you are right,
the Indians call all Nepalis Bahadurs as if they had no other names, and
    that's mistaken identity, but you have to admit that every time an
    American shakes my hand,
he or she has to pledge their love for Indian food and I can't even say I
    thank you
—on the behalf of Indian food. The repeated joke carries away his indignation
and as his wife waits to serve him the food she has cooked, your host provides
you space to note around him the wide measure of his Indian identity: the
    classical music of Pandit Jasraj, the distinguished books of literature,
    Tagore's fabulous art
—in their wealth irreducible to a plate of food, however rich.

There are small yellow flowers printed on her dress
and the flowers on her shoulders remain self-consciously stiff as she explains
on the Youth Hour on national television that men masturbate on her shoulder
in the buses choking with commuters on her way to school and she doesn't
      even
protest anymore because the clerks clutching their tiffins, the students, the
      housewives
from Daryaganj or Greater Kailash, numerous nurses, the blind, often in
      pairs, policemen who use their uniforms to avoid buying tickets, the offi-
      cers who get on at Boat Club, are all traveling along a singular line that
      links them to their goals in their
minds and any unpleasant diversions over the hardened penises of strange
      men
shoving themselves on the shoulders of school-girls trembling on their seats
are as noticeable as bumps on the capital-city's wide streets and you in your
      homes who are worried about mistaken identities will you please explain
      this one girl's
sudden desire to push the son-of-a-bitch driver aside and speed this bus
into the deepest waters and let the filth be cleansed forever.

The village school-teacher pushes his umbrella deeper into the earth
making a hole not big enough to swallow him as he listens to the eighteen-
year-old fisherman describe to the civil-rights lawyer that he had followed
      the crowd
as it went from house-to-house pillaging and burning, dumping in the wells
the bodies of the Muslims who were too slow, or weak, or plain stubborn,
or afraid, and maybe even too trusting, to run to the surrounding rice-fields,
and that he too, and he kneels into the dirty water to scoop up a tiny crab,
      took home
some stuff from those houses, actually a wooden window-frame and a cot,
and now it seems unlikely that the Muslims will return and maybe their lands
will be taken over by some of the Hindu farmers who can get the papers,
and later, as the school-teacher and the lawyer sit in the house of a Muslim
      landlord,
the old man explains that it isn't a case of mistaken identity that he had
      been spared,
it's simply that the villagers were afraid he had guns.

In London the visiting Korean and Japanese businessmen buy silk lingerie
in the shops behind Globe Theatre but he read recently that the Indians and
    Pakistanis
there have been paying thirty pounds a head to watch the lesbian double-act
of two Muslim girls, Zarina and Qumar, and what sort of mistaken identity
    is it
that makes him connect all that to the stories of transported loves
of a friend whose hands are small and brown like his mother's
telling him in a bar in New York that her current American boyfriend just
    asked her
when she'd get over her difference, she could not use her being Indian as an
    excuse, he said, the way people keep blaming the fact that their parents
    were alcoholics,
when in fact in trying to save her he is forgetting so much just like those
    Asian butchers who hacked a Muslim prostitute in Southall halal-style,
    letting her bleed to death,
and in any case it's excuse enough for his friend to declare her distance
from her love for this man who was pledging Sigma Chi in Michigan
while she was eating bhelpuri in Bombay.

Mistaken identity is not, however, a name that you can pin on
to the face of the anonymous killer on the notices put out by the police.
This question is like a new line you might draw on a map to link two places
in a relation that is yours. It is like snatching away the mask that the President
of your country wears when he plays golf and molding it into a toy for a child,
a shelter for the homeless, a fresh slogan for change or a poem about the
    future.
Naming only fixes you as one or the other, the substance or the shadow.
It is not enough to say that the worker who was killed was called Jeevan.
It is not enough to say that Jeevan was a worker at the Modi metal factory.
The point about mistaken identity is in a sense not about names at all:
its just about declaring that it is never enough. For if it were enough . . .

Against Nostalgia

They will not come back.
The smile on the lips of Safdar Hashmi.
The mornings
on the days just after the Emergency had ended.
My first green kite.
My sister's childhood.
The glitter of her diamond nose-ring
when Begum Akhtar sang.
The red *paan* she put in her mouth.
Bharat Coffee House on Fraser Road in Patna
where we ate masala dosa after watching *Sholay.*
The December afternoon when the last exams
were finally over and every geometry set was now forever useless.
The cricket commentary about G. R. Vishwanath's
wristy century at Chepauk.
In the summer afternoons
of Delhi when I was eighteen
the meeting of the New Wave
and the heat wave.
The flicker of anger on the screen of Om Puri's face.
A young snake taut
in the middle of the yellow dirt-road at noon.

They will not come back
even if you call them.
Not even the one whose leaving turned
all the leaves sere and brought winter to a barred door.

They will not come back.
The minute before Salman Rushdie
learned that there was a fatwa on his head.
The minute after
he had heard
that he was the winner of the Booker Prize.

They will not come back.
Your elder brother who died in a car accident.
Your younger sister only nineteen
who was too young to do much
much less to have taken her own life.

If they will not come back
we will have to take them in our hands
and place our thoughts of them
with great care near the open window
that faces the morning sun.
The mangoes
that were cheap and delicious
even though your father remembered them
being cheaper and more delicious still
in those days
that will not come back.
In those days before asthma and Cortisone
had changed the way your mother looked
at photographs of herself
holding you.

But I have never heard my mother
talk about the days
that she must know will never come back.
What sticks in her throat when she thinks about those days?

Calling
out to one
part of us from those days
in which before he became famous
people say Nusrat sang
at the roadside with *surma* in his eyes?

They were never there. Those days
that will never come back.

The days before television.
When there was only one Communist Party.
When you died in the house you were born in.
When you knew who was a Hindu and who a Muslim
and it did not matter.
They were never there. Those days.
Or even if they were
they were there only in the pages of history books.

Like the days when Megasthenes wrote
in his diary in 303 B.C.
that in Pataliputra
people left their doors unlocked.
He was writing in the light
of the oil lamp that left on the gold ceiling
adorned with nude sculptures
a layer of soot as black
as the kohl
in the eyes of the slave woman attending on him.

Those were the days
when people left their doors unlocked.
It is only the thieves today
who most loudly repeat the tale
of the Greek traveler in ancient India.

Those were the days
Megasthenes had written in his journal
as he lay in bed
gathering the kohl from the black eyes
of the slave woman
sent to him one night
in Pataliputra which is present-day Patna
where my mother cannot leave her doors unlocked.

Those were the days
that are not going to come back
when people left
the doors of their homes unlocked

—and those who didn't
have houses to lock
were never around to remind you
that those days will not come back.

What will come back
will be the yellow flowers of *amaltas*
stained with fresh dew.
What will come back are the times we will meet
at the end of long journeys.
What will come back
will come back with new possibilities
of hard defeat and hard-won victories.
What will come back
will be the songs of the striking fisherfolk
in a film by Anand Patwardhan.
What will come back will be the words
you had forgotten though you had always remembered the song.
What will come back again
is the need to cry
for that which never came back.
What will come back is the one who never left.

What will come back
among those who have left their homes
will be the new sounds of mutiny
among Asian bands in London.
What will come back are the posters
"In defence of our secular tradition"
brought from the Rafi Marg office of Sahmat.
What will come back even here
is rice and fish in mustard curry.
And stepping out of the dark skyscraper
into light a long-haired woman in a green sari.

What will come back are the promises
you pressed into the hands of those whose shadows
framed the doorways of your departure.
What will come back during evenings
like this one to haunt you are the poems
like friends who helped you understand
that there was no going back for any one of you.

SACHIN B. PATEL

Born in Gujarat, Sachin B. Patel moved to the United States when he was five. He graduated from Carleton College in Minnesota with a BA in English. Over the years he has performed alongside President Bill Clinton, made a short film, and helped initiate an annual community performing arts event in Minneapolis. Patel received the Joseph Collins Foundations Scholarship for his essay "Through the Microscope of Humanity," and as a writer and activist, his works have appeared in *Mizna* and in the anthology *Body Language: Poems of the Medical Training Experience* (BOA Editions Ltd., 2006). He currently practices internal and critical care medicine and lives in North Carolina with his wife, Laura.

> *Through ten childhood migrations, it was living and working in a*
> *"Patel Motel" that rooted my Desiamericanism.*

In the Business of Erasing History

A delicate spray of dilute Simple Green on the motel bed stand.
Tight circular motions that remove
puddles of lust surrounding traces of lipstick—vanish.
The bed sheets: starched gossamer on which a child was accidentally
    conceived—perhaps.

A wave of Clorox cascading down the tub,
wiping away the epiphany from a cathartic bath.
The tub: where candlelight inspired metaphors,
Dissolving the nebulous delusions of a poet on the cusp of brilliance—
    maybe.

A steady hum of a Hoover, as its harmonic motion
inhales pebbles from Tybee Island, soil from Morgantown, or grass from
    Tillsonburg.
The carpet: the only witness as two masked men planned an exotic getaway,
after liberating cash from the local 7-Eleven—possibly.

Day after day, the pillows are set upright,
the furniture is arranged symmetrically,
and the smells are neutralized.
The slate is wiped clean—again and again.
We are in the business
of spraying, removing, scrubbing, and vacuuming—erasing.

We are in the business
of erasing history.

The Blacktop Gospels

Bombarded with contusions in my dyslexic middle school pimple-hood,
I grew accustomed—to *less than great* expectations.
Back then, we lived on the outer rim of W. Philadelphia,
where the schism between country clubs and housing projects,
was like the viper-tongued rhetoric
of seventh grade girls.

Whose ponytailed bourgeoisities bred
blasphemous thoughts of cultural inferiority
in my membrane,
silencing my mother tongue * [shhh!]

                                                in the presence of pink schoolmates.

I mean, when my *Mother* would call for me to come to dinner, "*Beta, Jumva
   aaow!*"
my *ears would deafen,*
and I would shrink
to Lilliputian proportions,
hoping that my Gulliver-sized playmate
wouldn't shake his blond head in disgust.
Disgusted by the otherness
Of a kid who would *always* be a filthy foreigner,
even as a polished hand surgeon
with a bachelor's in English Lit.

As neurons begin to divide and conquer
my notions of reality,
feelings of arrested development,
weave in and out of my desire to confabulate the truth,
and tell freckled Jenny Harrigan in Mrs. McQuade's math class,
that, yes, indeed, my father worked nights,
because he was a famous cardiologist,
when in reality he manned
the decaying, bullet-holed 7–Eleven on Dekalb Pike.
How he filled cherry slurpies,
when he should have been transfusing el sangre.

A black-bearded man who couldn't anticipate
the binladinbullshit about to shred his sacred turban to rags.

But he remains . . . persists . . . sticks
in the corners of your mouth
like that *"authentic hummus you love to buy at the co-op."*

But, like a turtle shrinking into his shell,
I cowered in the back of class,
and watched Jenny hand out valentines,
to all the boys . . . who were blond.
My puffy black hair just couldn't compare, I guess.
Unable to understand why Tom Selleck's
dark mustache made him so sexy
and my 12 year-old peach fuzz a sideshow,
     I grabbed my Spalding,
     and dribbled toward the Courts,
     searching for answers.

Now *here* the blacktop paved a *new reality.*
And past ballers became legends,
imparting wisdom upon the youth.
Older ballers kept tabs on us,
making sure we did our homework and said our prayers . . .

"cuz, listen up, little bigman," Dre would say,
"school and faith, are the only things that'll save you in this world."

And so it came to pass that I was baptized
on the basketball courts of West Philly,
where Fonso and Cass showed a brotha
the bouncing ball gospels of the old school.

"Don't be afraid to take it up strong, kid . . . with dignity."

On the court is where I had my communion.
An education about the lopsided reality
of an America too pale to comprehend it's own hypocritical imperialism.

"I mean, like really, Brittany, why do all these Hindoos smell like curry?"

"Son," *Crossover Tesh* would say,
"don't you pay her no mind,
after all isn't that why they pay
12 dollars and change to slurp down
the brown funk at *Delights of India?*
Because then, they can say they've been
to an *authentic* "Indian" restaurant,
and you *know* cocktail party pakoras
can't come close to your Momma's culinary virtuosity."

Back on the courts in '91
we never thought that George Bush would become a sequel.

The gurus of the court tried to break it down for us . . .
cuz we couldn't understand

why the sand-niggers about to be
bombed by oil company heads
were the mirror images of our fathers . . .
who *AREN'T* in heaven cuz heaven ain't fo' heathens.

Ahh! I'm Confused, Desillused, and slightly bruised:

[*breath*] that's when, *Fade-away Mo* the Pakistani poet-baller would say,
      "*Boy, if you feel like shit,*
      it's because you're becoming browner
      than you've ever been before."

Learning . . . understanding . . .
that you don't have to be Schizophrenic
To be delusional in this society.

  . . . Mixed messages of constipated identity
being flushed out in Ex-Lax proportions.
Cleansing me . . . from the inside-out.

"to the ticktock you don't stopstop, to the ticktock you don't stopstop . . ."

LaTrinko, the flamboyant Russian beat boxer,
would hook it up w/ a little sumthin' sumthin'
to grease those pump*fakes.*

We had hip/hop, hip to the hop.
As we watched the colored girls sit on the grass
by the court fabricating forbidden
erotica about their favorite *chocolate superstar.*

Cuz for LaRonda and Tamika,
the rainbow was *not enough,*
and they pumped our egos,

with ghetto bootieshakes
and dangling hooprings.

. . . But *OH!* a fast break,
three on two,
Skywalker Sanjay whizzes down the lane . . .

and ssssoars, like a royal falcon,
untouchably high,
a cinnamon-skinned comet
inspiring awe, in pubescent émigrés
from various motherlands.

Now, *that boy* . . . was a hero,
to banish the ground beneath
his feet and . . . * up. up. and *away* to the clouds,
where saxophone concertos
freshened the warm April breeze,
and regal trumpets welcomed
his highness to a world that can be.

That will be,
when we stop cowering in complacency . . . and dare to inspire.

BUSHRA REHMAN

Born and raised in New York City, Bushra Rehman has also lived in Pakistan and Saudi Arabia. She is the coeditor of *Colonize This! Young Women of Color on Today's Feminism* (Seal Press, 2002) and the author of the poetry collection *Marianna's Beauty Salon* (Vagabond Press, 2001). Her work has appeared in publications such as the *New York Times, India Currents, NY Newsday, ColorLines, Curve,* and *SAMAR,* and anthologies such as *Voices of Resistance: Muslim Women on War, Faith and Sexuality* (Seal Press, 2006), and *Stories of Illness and Healing: Women Write Their Bodies* (Kent State University Press, 2007). Her work has also been featured on BBC Radio 4, the *Brian Lehrer Show,* and KPFA radio. She has just completed her first work of fiction, an on-the-road Desi adventure novel.

> *I'm a Pakistani from Queens, New York City, with roots in North-West Frontier Province, underneath the waters of the Tarbela Dam.*

Ami's Cassettes

The other day, I found my mother's cassettes from the eighties
they were full of love songs from Indian movies
Ami used to tape them from the TV while she cleaned

And I thought back to the orange carpets
the sofas with their plastic
the way everything was dusted and perfect

I tried to fill the memory with her music
to come up with something peaceful,
something splendid
but the tapes they just didn't play that way

You see, they caught all the background noise:
the sound of babies crying
children fighting

fire engines going
and then the sound of a child being hit

The children wouldn't stop making noise
until my mother's own voice would break
then there would be nothing
but the sound of her crying
and the sound of music
in a language
my mother was dying to hear

I thought back to the orange carpets
the way that I would press my face against them
and against the plastic sofas
until the perspiration would make it stick
and listen to the sound of her crying
and all the love songs of longing
they promised everything
missing in that house
with its orange carpets
everything missing in the plastic
everything she ever recorded.

At the Museum of Natural History

As we both look up at the Tyrannosaurus Rex
its bones painted black, its danger extinct
I can hear the sounds of children echo
throughout the museum

And we are not afraid this way
to stand a few inches away from each other

We are not afraid because it's over
The Tyrannosaurus Rex does not scare us
We don't scare each other

It's over, the bones are beginning to fade
and bleach in our failure

But if one day someone finds our remains
and decides to lay them right next to each other
will they lay them in their proper ways
will they mix up my hip with yours
will they place the fingers of my hands
on someone else's palms

Will they ever know
this flesh answered the other
that my fingers traveled all over
the empty space around your bones

The Difference

It's the difference between
whether you talk to the girl or not
whether you carry the moon home
in the seat of your pants
Burning and cool
ready to lay it on your tongue
in the privacy of your room
and let its holy light burn through
your blood
Or whether you walk home
with the moon in your stomach
heavy as a rock
With all the sidewalks pulling you down
and all the well-lit buildings
of a midtown night winking on and off
Saying we know you, you're the one who
goes home alone and types in the dark
with the small cut of your window
always blocking the light of the moon off

SHAILJA PATEL

The first South Asian and Kenyan to compete at the national level in U.S. slam poetry contests, Shailja Patel was the Lambda National Slam Champion 2003 and featured in *Bullets and Butterflies: A Queer Slam Anthology* (Suspect Thoughts Press, 2005). She is the author of two poetry chapbooks: *Dreaming In Gujarati* and *Shilling Love*. Her one-woman spoken word theater show, *Migritude,* has toured globally; received commissions from the Ford Foundation, the National Performance Network, and the Nairobi World Social Forum; and was short-listed for Italy's Camaiore Prize 2009. Her awards include the inaugural Fanny-Ann Eddy Poetry Award from IRN-Africa, the Voices of Our Nations Poetry Award, an Innovative Talent Award from Indian American Women Empowered, and the Outwrite Poetry Prize of the New York Lesbian and Gay Centre. Patel was the 2009 guest writer at the Nordic Africa Institute, Sweden.

> *I am a radical Desi internationalist, pan-Africanist, feminist, and live in Nairobi and the San Francisco Bay Area.*

Shilling Love

One

They never said / they loved us

Those words were not / in any language / spoken by my parents

I love you honey was the dribbled caramel / of Hollywood movies / Dallas / Dynasty / where hot water gushed / at the touch of gleaming taps / electricity surged / 24 hours a day / through skyscrapers banquets obscene as the Pentagon / were mere backdrops / where emotions had no consequences words / cost nothing meant nothing would never / have to be redeemed

My parents / didn't speak / that / language

1975 / 15 Kenyan shillings to the British pound / my mother speaks battle

Storms the bastions of Nairobi's / most exclusive prep schools / hurls our cowering / six-year old bodies like cannonballs / into the all-white classrooms / scales the ramparts of class distinction / around Loreto convent / where the president / sends his daughter / the foreign diplomats / send their daughters / because my mother's daughters / will / have world-class educations

She falls / regroups / falls and re-groups / in endless assaults on visa officials / who sneer behind their bulletproof windows / at US and British consulates / my mother the general / arms her daughters / to take on every citadel

1977 / 20 Kenyan shillings to the British pound / my father speaks / stoic endurance /
he began at 16 the brutal apprenticeship / of a man who takes care of his own / relinquished dreams of / pilot rally driver for the daily crucifixion / of wringing profit from underneath cars / my father the foot soldier, bound to an honor / deeper than any currency / *you must / finish what you start you must / march until you drop you must / give your life for those / you bring into the world*

I try to explain love / in shillings / to those who've never gauged / who gets to leave who has to stay / who breaks free and what they pay / those who've never measured love / by every rung of the ladder / from survival / to choice

A force as grim and determined / as a boot up the backside / a spur that draws blood /
a mountaineer's rope / that yanks / relentlessly / up

My parents never say / they love us / they save and count / count and save / the shilling falls against the pound / college fees for overseas students / rise like flood tides / love is a luxury / priced in hard currency / ringed by tariffs

/ and we devour prospectuses / of ivied buildings smooth lawns vast /
libraries the way Jehovah's witnesses / gobble visions of paradise / because
we know we'll have to be /

twice as good three times as fast four times as driven / with angels powers
and principalities on our side just / to get / on / the / plane
Thirty shillings to the pound forty shillings to the pound / my parents fight
over money late in the night / my father pounds the walls and yells / *I
can't—it's impossible—what do you think I am?* / My mother propels us
through school tuition exams applications / locks us into rooms to study /
keeps an iron grip on the bank books

1982 / gunshots / in the streets of Nairobi / military coup leaders / thunder
over the radio / Asian businesses wrecked and looted Asian women raped /
after / the government / regains control / we whisper what the coup leaders
planned

Round up all the Asians at gunpoint / in the national stadium / strip them of
what / they carry / march them 30 miles / elders in wheelchairs / babies in
arms / march them 30 miles to the airport / pack them onto any planes / of
any foreign airline / tell the pilots / down the rifle barrels / *leave* / *we don't
care where you take them* / *leave*

I learn like a stone in my gut that / third-generation Asian Kenyan will
never / be Kenyan enough / all my patriotic fervor / will never turn my skin
black / as yet another western country / drops a portcullis / of immigration
spikes / my mother straps my shoulders back with a belt / to teach me / to
stand up straight

50 Kenyan shillings to the pound / we cry from meltdown pressure / of
exam after exam where second place is never good enough / they snap /
faces taut with fear / *you can't be soft* / *you have to fight* / *or the world will eat
you up*

75 Kenyan shillings to the pound / they hug us / tearless stoic at airports / as
we board planes for icy alien England / cram instructions into our pockets

like talismans / *Eat proper meals so you don't get sick* / *cover your ears against the cold* / *avoid those muffathias* / *the students without purpose or values* / *learn and study* / *succeed* / *learn and study* / *succeed* / *remember remember remember the cost of your life*

they never say / they love us

Two

I watch how I love / I admonish exhort / like a Himalayan guide I / rope my chosen ones / yank them remorselessly up / when they don't even want to be / on the frigging mountain

like a vigilante squad I / scan dark streets for threats I / strategize for war and famine I / slide steel down spines

I watch heat / steam off my skin / when Westerners drop / *I love you* into conversation / like blueberries hitting / soft / muffin dough / I convert it to shillings / and I wince

December 2000 / 120 shillings to the British pound / 90 Kenyan shillings to the US dollar / my sister Sneha and I / wait for our parents / at SFO's international terminal

Four hours after / their plane landed / they have not emerged

And we know with the hopeless rage / of third-world citizens / African passport holders / that the sum of their lives and labor / dreams and sacrifice / was measured sifted weighed found / wanting / by the INS Somewhere deep in the airport's underbelly / in a room rank with fear and despair / my parents / who have traveled / 27 hours / across three continents / to see their children / are interrogated / by immigration officials

My father the footsoldier / numb with exhaustion / is throwing away / all the years / with reckless resolve / telling them / *take the passports* / *take them* / *stamp them* / *no readmission EVER* / *just let me out to see my daughters*

My mother the general / dizzy with desperation / cuts him off shouts him down /
demands *listen to me I'm the one / who filled in the visa forms* / in her mind her lip curls
she thinks / *these Americans / call themselves so advanced so / modern but still / in the year 2000 / they think it must be the husband in charge / they won't let the wife speak*

On her face a lifetime / of battle-honed skill and charm / turns like a heat lamp / onto the INS man until he / stretches / yawns / relents / he's tired / it's late / he wants his dinner / and my parents / trained from birth / to extend Indian / hospitality / open their bags and offer their sandwiches / to this man / who would have sent them back / without a thought

Sneha and I / in the darkened lobby / watch the empty exit way / our whole American / dream-bought-with-their-lives / hisses mockery around our rigid bodies / we swallow sobs because / they raised us to be tough / they raised us to be fighters and into that / clenched haze / of not / crying

here they come

hunched / over their luggage carts our tiny / fierce / fragile / dogged / indomitable parents

Hugged tight they stink / of 31 hours in transit / hugged tighter we all stink / with the bravado of all the years / pain bitten down on gargantuan hopes / holding on through near-disasters / never ever / giving in / to softness

The stench rises off us / unbearable / of what / was never said

Something / is bursting the walls of my arteries something / is pounding its way up my throat like a volcano / rising / finally / I understand / why I'm a poet
Because I was born to a law / that states / before you claim a word you steep it / in terror and shit / in hope and joy and grief / in labor endurance vision costed out / in decades of your life / you have to sweat and curse it / pray

and keen it / crawl and bleed it / with the very marrow / of your bones / you
have to earn / its / meaning

Love Poem for London

The night Youssou N'Dour
sang at the South Bank
cicadas shrieked for joy
in Stockwell's streets
gargoyles jumped off Westminster Abbey
to bump and grind in alleyways.

The night Ravi Shankar
played sitar at Albert Hall
queer Asian boys with kohl-rimmed eyes
danced bhangra in the lanes of Brixton
saffron sashes at their wrists and hips.

The night the Japanese theater company
played A Midsummer Night's Dream
in the shadow of St. Paul's Cathedral
boneless Tokyo acrobats
cartwheeled across Covent Garden
Oberon and Titania swept the Strand
in satin kimono embroidered like gardens
Helena wept exquisite porcelain tears
into the Thames.

Fairies donkeys
gamboled Embankment
whispered into autumn wind
if we spirits have offended
think but this and all is mended
if we spirits have offended . . . . . .

You kissed frangipani
round my wrists
I planted Nandi flame
along your spine
jasmine bloomed
beneath my skin
under your lips.

We leapt for red buses
flew into windstreams
gravity-free
bodies spun midair.

The night voices of Senegal
ran molten gold into the Thames
speedboats turned to clove-laden dhows
trade winds belled their sails
ice cubes clinked into cowrie shells
across the city's wine bars.

The night the edges of London
flowed out to passionate raags
silver anklets on disembodied feet
jingled dandia rhythms
down Whitehall.

Police truncheons fruited nectarines
tear gas canisters burped out
green coriander clouds
Hyde Park squirrels flashed neon orange
tree to tree like northern lights
banana trees exploded
greenhouse walls in Kew
coffee bushes flung
red berries to the swans.

We feasted on falafel in Trafalgar Square
sitting on bronze lions
under Nelson's stare, cars a crazy
headlamp-dance around our centrifuge.

You said
Paris?
I said
forget it
you offered the Seine
I said
French nuclear tests in the Pacific
you whispered
Champs Elysées
I snarled
racist visa policies
you murmured
Provence
I said
Jean Le-Pen
you painted romance
I parried with politics.

We were both right
and we were both wrong
making a poem
we hadn't a shape for
layering improvised harmonies
onto an unscored page.

You licked hummus
off my fingers
which is one way
to win an argument.

N'dour sang richest red
laterite dust
into our nostrils
Shankar silvered nets of raags
around the shoals of London boroughs
stockbrokers stirred
in brandied dreams
woke to sandalwood crumbs
rain-insect wings
on their pillows.

The night Shakespeare's midsummer madness
became forever Japanese
Puck backflipped
through bush through briar
heartbreak and truth
through flood through fire
illusion and mischief
I do wander everywhere
swifter than a moon's sphere.

We all served the fairy queen that night.
London lay at our feet
Omani carpet Kashmiri shawl
symphony we entered
your woodwind my percussion
story with a subplot
shaped exactly like us.

I was electric you incandescent
my hair shot sparks your breath ignited.

SUDEEP SEN

Sudeep Sen studied at Columbia University's Journalism School and was a visiting scholar at Harvard. He won the Hawthornden Fellowship (UK) and was nominated for a Pushcart Prize for poems featured in *Postmarked India: New and Selected Poems* (HarperCollins India, 1997). Other books include *Distracted Geographies* (Wings Press, 2003), *Rain* (Mapin/Gallerie, 2006), *Aria* (Yeti/Mulfran, 2009), *Blue Nude: Poems and Translations 1977–2012* (forthcoming), and *The HarperCollins Book of New English Poetry by Indians* (2010). His writings have appeared in the *Times Literary Supplement,* the *Guardian,* the *Independent,* the *Harvard Review,* and *India Today.* His work has been broadcast on BBC, CNN-IBN, and NDTV and anthologized in *New Writing 15* (Granta, 2007), *Indian Love Poems* (Knopf/Random House/Everyman, 2005), and *Language for a New Century: Contemporary Poetry from Asia, the Middle East and Beyond* (W. W. Norton, 2008). Recently, he edited the *Literary Review: The Indian Poetry Issue* (2009). He is the editorial director of AARK ARTS and the editor of *Atlas.*

I am a transnational writer with New York being one of my significant anchors. My writing is influenced by Indian, European, and American traditions, both classical and modern.

Offering

the kindness of libation, lyric, and blood—

her endless notes left for me—
                little secrets, graces—
        trills recorded on blue and purple parchment
to be lipped, tasted, devoured—

only the essence remains—
        its stickiness, its juice, its memory—

seamless juxtaposition—
    the brute and the passion,
        dry of the bone and wet of the sea,
coarseness of the page and smooth of the nib's iridium

I try and trace a line, a very long line—

    the ink blots
        as this line's linear edge
dissolves and frays—

like capillary threads
    gone mad
        twirling in the deep heat of the tropics—

threads unraveling,
    each sinew tense with the want of moisture
and the other's flesh—

there are no endings here—
only beginnings—
        precious incipience—

translucent drops of sweat
    perched precariously on her collar-bone
        waiting to slide,
roll unannounced into the gulleys
that yearn to soak in the rain—

heart-beat shift
the shape of globules
    as they alter their balance and color,
changing their very point of gravity—

constantly deceiving the other—

I stand, wanting—
        wanting more of the bone's dry edge,
the infinite blur of desire,
                                the dream,
        the wet, the salt, the ink,
and   the underside of her skin—

Jacket on a Chair

You carelessly tossed
    the jacket on a chair.
The assembly of cloth

    collapsed in slow motion
into a heap of cotton—
    cotton freshly picked

from the fields—
    like flesh
without a spine.

    The chair's wooden
frame provided a brief
    skeleton,

but it wasn't enough
    to renew the coat's
shape, the body's

    prior strength,
or the muscle
    to hold its own.

When one peels off
    one's outer skin,
it is difficult

   to hide
the true nature of
   blood.

Wood, wool, stitches,
   and joints—
an epitaph

   of a cardplayer's
shuffle,
   and the history

of my dark faith.

[based on Cezanne's *Jacket on a Chair,* graphite and watercolor
on paper, 47.5 X 30.5 cm, 1890–92]

AIMEE NEZHUKUMATATHIL

Aimee Nezhukumatathil is the author of *At the Drive-In Volcano* (Tupelo Press, 2007), winner of the Balcones Prize, and *Miracle Fruit* (2003), which received the Tupelo Press Prize, the *ForeWord Magazine* Book of the Year Award in poetry, and the Global Filipino Award. Recent awards for her writing include an NEA fellowship in poetry and the Pushcart Prize. Her poetry and essays have been widely anthologized and have appeared in *180 More: Extraordinary Poems for Every Day* (Random House, 2005) and *Language for a New Century: Poetry from the Middle East, Asia and Beyond* (W. W. Norton, 2008). She is an associate professor of English at State University New York (SUNY) at Fredonia, where she was awarded a Chancellor's Medal of Excellence and the Hagan Young Scholars Award. She lives with her husband and son in western New York.

> *My mother is from the Philippines, and my father is from Kerala.*
> *They met in Chicago, where I was born, and I'm grateful to have this*
> *delicious blend of cultures informing my life and my work.*

The Mascot of Beavercreek High Breaks Her Silence

There are some suits more difficult to remove:
spades, armor, tweed in the summer, light, cups.
Those nights you thought I was home, dateless, studying
for chemistry, memorizing the dates of epic battles—

I worked myself into a lather of sweat for a field
of angry young men. Sometimes they were so close
I could feel their hot breath in the space between my head
and furry neck. Even the captain of the cheerleaders

never went that far. Every hand that once reached
for me still haunts me at the most unexpected times:
as I place vegetables on the grocery belt, or walking
the glow-wall walkway at the Detroit airport.

Something still pulls me to the ground and it's not
the crowd, the scent of cola and popcorn, the tinge
of engine grease, or a truck revving at Homecoming.
If you slice a jacaranda bloom between two glass slides

and place it on a microscope, the corolla will always fight
for the light. If you once posed for any pictures
with me, still have them scattered somewhere in an attic,
look carefully at the dark netting of my mouth.

If you squint hard, you can see my actual teeth,
clenched into a small scream. I was like that every night.
It was high school, after all. I was always cheering
for something. Still am. Something is always worth

cheering for. There is always some cheer
worth something. Cheer for some worth, always.

Fishbone

At dinner, my mother says if one gets stuck
 in your throat, roll some rice into a ball
and swallow it whole. She says things
like this and then the next thing out of her mouth

is *did you know Madonna is pregnant?*
But I want to ponder the basket of fried smelt
on the table, lined with paper towels to catch
 the grease—want to study their eyes

like flat soda, wonder how I'm supposed
to eat them whole. Wonder why we can't
have normal food for breakfast like at Sara's house—
Cheerios, or sometimes if her mother is home:

buttered toast and soft-boiled eggs
in her grandmother's dainty blue egg cups
and matching blue spoon. Safe. Pretty.
Nothing with eyes. Under the flakes of fried crust,

I see a shimmer of skin as silver as foil,
like the dimes my mother tapes to a board
for each year I'm alive. How she tucked this
into my suitcase before I left for college

and I forgot about '93 and '95. How she said
she'll never find a '93, and shouldn't this
be a great thing to one day put into an oak frame,
but not now, not until we find the missing coin?

How we don't have many traditions left, thanks
to Your Father. These are the things she says
instead of a blessing to our food. These are the words
that stick inside me as I snap off the next head.

Last Aerogramme to You, With Lizard

Kovalam, India

I found a bat today—its belly full of bloody mosquitoes.
If I squint, the shoreline of coconut trees becomes green star
lights strung across a patio. On the other side of this window

you and our dog sleep on packed bright earth. Follow
the leggy cats in this village, some curled up in bars
tucked up in tea and smoke. Newspapers here report callow

boys sneaking into nearby huts with machetes—all for easy dough
to finger in the sweaty pockets of their jeans. Can you smell the cigars
in this place? I sit on one of the boys' spinning chairs—some fellow

still warms me and it's not you, not even a nicked photo
of us ankle-deep in a lake I swore was full of snakes. The sandbar
sinks lower when I try to walk across, so I spread my toes

for extra balance. I have followed you for years, sent jumbo-
sized letters smudged and slicked down, but this I *swear*
is the last aerogramme to you. Now even my saliva glows

in the dark. Cats pool near the bed but I know there is one gecko
left to thrill my sleep. I know it won't bite, but the bizarre
way it skitters a loop around my wrist—exploring each elbow—
makes me weep for you. My cheek is wet. A lizard makes it so.

Mr. Mustard's Dance Club: Ladies Night

Seventeen, but we breezed right by the bouncers—
Me and Jill in tight tee-shirts and Levi's, flannel shirts

wrapped at our small waists. We danced together,
(never with boys) never drank, even when boys

offered to buy. Once, after I refused a beer, I heard
one say, "You know, them Asians can do

all those bending things." And I wondered *what*
bending things, what this had to do with taking

a sip from a cold bottle I didn't purchase. Still, we danced
to *Culture Club, Madonna, Men at Work, Bananarama*—

music we grew up with, heavy with keyboards
and drum machines. Our hairlines grew damp,

wisps of baby hair pulled loose from my ponytail.
Jill spied a water cooler by the phones and plucked

paper cones down for each of us to pour coolness,
to pour questions about people who bend.

RAVI CHANDRA

Having graduated from Brown University with a degree in biology, Ravi Chandra subsequently attended Stanford Medical School. He now practices psychiatry at a community mental health clinic, where he serves predominantly an Asian and Russian immigrant population, and is also in private practice. He was awarded first prize in a poetry contest at Stanford Medical Center, which also published his poetry in its chapbook. Slam poetry then became his passion, and he was an alternate on the 2002 San Francisco Slam Team. He is involved with the biennial Asian Pacific Islander American Poetry Summit. He lives in San Francisco, where he writes a blog, "Memoirs of a Superfan," for the International Asian American Film Festival.

I find affinity with people of many diasporas in the San Francisco Bay Area while being rooted as a South Asian American.

Cleanup on Aisle #3

Why is it that every kind of person out there
has their counterpart in food?
No matter if the skin's bleached or baked
epicanthus blepharoplastied
turning almond eyes to permanently shocked lychee-size—
Let's face it, when your
exterior complexion
doesn't match
your interior direction
you're on the menu for racial epicurification.

The oreo was the original food slur:
a nicer way to symbolize the person whose insides
(and insights)
didn't match their stand-out outsides.

Banana wasn't far behind, for those who
weren't bananas about their yellow hue.

And Coconuts, I hate to say, might look like me,
but their brains are pure white matter.

But before I got too down on the whiter persuasion,
I met first one hardboiled egg,
then a dozen,

and wondered a time or two, if I wasn't
a Tea Egg (brown on the outside, golden on the inside) after all, or
a Sweet Potato (brown on the outside, buddhist on the inside)
or just a plain Reese's Peanut Butter Cup,
always in search of a Hershey's Hug (I'll settle for a Kiss),
a Mint Chocolate Drop (a sweet brown girl who joined the Greens),
a Juicy Peach (a soft and fuzzy Buddhist with a hard center)
(that could break your teeth)
(I would say a Mango, but that mongo seed kinda scares me)
or even an Avocado (an ecologist that could break your teeth),
Vegetarian Hot Pocket or Three Cheese Bagel Bite
(don't even ask)

Yes, I'll admit it—
I've spent hours in Safeway aisles
just trying
to figure out what or who I am
—call it Existential Hunger—
only to realize that no matter what you look like,
it's what's inside that counts.
Which is why I'm a Scrambled Egg Burrito
in a Tomato Tortilla
with Black Beans, Basmati Rice, Guacamole, and Sriracha
garnished with Sweet Papaya Chutney
with a side of Bitter Melon.

I'm good with tongues, I don't break teeth,
your stomach might not agree with me,
and your nose won't know me—
but I'm nutritious,
guaranteed,
and I'm

      on
your
          plate.

Your eyes have never seen a dish like me before,
and I'm not just for breakfast,
anymore!

The Old Man Speaks

Mr. Wise, room 243
status post trauma (felled by a tree)
stilled by broken bones, packed in plaster,
cracked ribs, collapsed lung (arboreal disaster);
a hollow spear pierces his side
and the wall sucks blood and air
from him into a gurgling box
like the devil drawing on some infernal hookah
until his breath returns.

"Tomorrow," I say, "the tube comes out."
He nods, silently, and blinks, once
as I check his chart, his lungs, his heart
and then idly ask, making conversation,
"What kind of tree was it?"
He smiles, eyes bright
(his gaze goes through me)
"Apple," he whispers. "It
was *beautiful*."

RALPH NAZARETH

Originally from Mangalore, India, Ralph Nazareth graduated from Bombay University before receiving his doctorate in English literature from SUNY at Stony Brook. Nazareth has presented papers at Harvard, Yale, Princeton, and Columbia and published poems in journals such as *Christianity & Literature* and the *South Asian Literary Review*. He is currently a professor at Nassau Community College and the managing editor of Yuganta Press in Stamford, Connecticut.

> *A Mangalorean Catholic, I pray in Konkani, count in Kannada, swear in Tulu, sing in Hindi, write in English, and dream in American.*

A Question for Vaclav Havel

I see him in there by the sidewalk window sipping a caffè latte à la bruge, this wooden statesman with a heart and a nose that shows no sign of ever growing long. I dive in. And since you don't ask a President, even in a café, a question to his face, I grab a paper napkin and scribble with the magic marker used to write the Specials of the Day, "Do you think poetry can save the world?" and slide it across the table.

A bit of water on the glass top smudges my note as he picks up the question with a friendly smile and reaches into his breast pocket for his half-moon reading glasses. He reads my words with the solemnity we've come to expect from this former absurdist turned grave man of global vision.

He sighs as he re-folds the napkin. The shadow of a thought crosses his creased, pixie face. "Hmm, I've never thought of it," he says. "Now come to think of it, we wouldn't be here if not for pottery. Pottery is what has made us who we are," he adds. "We needed to be able to move away from the water's edge," he proceeds in a presidential drone. "It's pottery," he asserts, "that helped us to get to higher ground. You see, without pots we'd be—

how d'you say it in American—sitting ducks! I say that with deference to your Kansas Board of Education. Didn't they just kill the monkey in us?" he asks with a wink, and concludes, "But yes, I'd say, sure, there's a future in pottery."

Then rising and grasping me by the arm, he says, breaking into a grin, "Let us go then, you and I, and throw a pot!"

Red Eye

In the curved blue jeweled space,
the reading lamplight floods the narrow seat next to mine.
A man with the wise profile of Cyrus the Great
moves his finger purposefully along lines written in Farsi.
Now and then he invokes God's blessings on my sneezes
issuing with the plosive hiss of curses,
and then returns to the script I sense is hidden revelation.

There must be others here flying east in this pocket of darkness
whose lips are sealed over foreign tongues like ours,
hearts locked with the secrets of their native realms,
minds silently working out strategies of survival,
flecks of feelings percolating privately,
crisscrossed fingers and visions resting under blankets
warm with the gold wings of the TWA insignia.

In this sleek shuttle of the night,
poised to pierce the water light of embryonic dawn,
travelers all, stewards of the earth, we dream red-eyed.
He alone keeps vigil with the lines which move unmoving
through the shivering of the plane
and seem to breathe, "Stay awake, stay awake,
so you may know the beginning and end of things."

Horse Play

When we read about Bucephalus,
my son was four and together
we strode across the carpet plains,
sweeping, conquering worlds
the stallion in his veins leading
the older steed in mine

Sated, I tried to curb his onward thrust
his wanderlust and thirst for gain
but he was unstoppable until
he reined in on the Indus bank,
in fact, the east bay window sill,
the very edge of what was known to him.
Rising beside this hoary river
my Hindu forebears, awesome shades,
massed in girth of heavy hanging drapes
trumpeted world-haunting wails
reclaiming their long lost kin.

Bucephalus bucked and spilled
the little rider on the rug.
I took him up in my arms
this fallen fond imperator
and walked with him along the shore.
"Here I was born," I said,
"and, look, this is my ancient home."
"So?" he questioned in commanding tone
and raising his finger, fearsome sword,
declared, in words that were his own,

"All mine."

MEENA ALEXANDER

Meena Alexander was born in India and raised there and in Sudan; she went for further studies to England. Alexander's six volumes of poetry include *Quickly Changing River* (2008), *Raw Silk* (2004) and *Illiterate Heart* (2002, winner of the PEN Open Book Award), all published by TriQuarterly Books/ Northwestern University Press. She is the editor of *Indian Love Poems* (Everyman's Library/Knopf, 2005) and the author of *The Shock of Arrival: Reflections on Postcolonial Existence* (South End Press, 1997) and *Poetics of Dislocation* (University of Michigan Press, 2009). She has also published two novels, two works of literary criticism, and a memoir. Alexander is the recipient of fellowships from the John Simon Guggenheim, Fulbright, and Rockefeller foundations, the National Endowment for the Humanities, and the Arts Council of England. A long-time resident of Manhattan, she is a distinguished professor of English at Hunter College and CUNY Graduate Center.

I write in English—the rhythms of my mother tongue Malayalam, as well as Hindi, Arabic, and French, flow into my lines.

River and Bridge

Trees on the other side of the river
So blue, discarding light into water, a flat
White oil tank with HESS in black, a bridge
Holzer might skim with lights—I will take her
Down before she feels the fear—no sarcophagus here:

I have come to the Hudson's edge to begin my life
To be born again, to seep as water might
In a landscape of mist, burnished trees,
A bridge that seizes crossing.

But Homer knew it and Vyasa too, black river
And bridge summon those whose stinging eyes

Crisscross red lights, metal implements,
Battlefields: birth is always bloody.

September Sunlight

For Shuntaro Tanikawa

A woman in army castoffs
goes down the steps to the river.
A dove flutters each shoulder bone.
Here Seiji, here Setsuko, she murmurs.
Stay brother sun, stay sister moon.
Not so long ago in Hiroshima
woman in kimono, bird, and cloud
turned to shadows staining the ground.
Through branches of the sun
I watch her go down the steps to the river.
Her shadow brushes the lilac tree.
The birds are naked as birds well might be,
they sing to no one in particular.

Color of Home

From the poem cycle "Listening to Lorca"

I met you by Battery Park where the bridge once was.
Invisible it ran between the towers.
What made you follow me, O ghost in black cutaways?

Dear Mr. Lorca I address you,
filled with a formal feeling.
You were tongue tied on the subway till a voice cried out:

Thirty-fourth Street, last stop on the D.
It's the Empire State, our tallest again,
time to gather personal belongings, figure out redemption.

You leaned into my ribs muttering:
Did you hear that, you seller of salt
and gatherer of ash just as your foremothers were?

How the world goes on and on.
Have you ever seen a bullfight?
What do you have strapped to your back?

Then, quieter, under your breath:
Let's survive the last stop together.
I knew a Hindu ballerina once,

nothing like you, a quick, delicate thing.
I walked with her by the river
those months when English fled from me

and the young men of Manhattan
broke cherry twigs and scribbled on my skin
till one cried out—I am the boy killed by dark water,

surely you know me?
Then bolt upright you whispered:
Why stay on this island?

See how it's ringed by water and flame?
You who have never seen Granada—
tell me, what is the color of home?

Slow Dancing

From the poem cycle "Letters to Gandhi"

Dear Mr. Gandhi
please say something
about the carnage in your home state.

How did you feel when they shut
the gates of Sabarmati Ashram
that February night

and the wounded clung outside?
What has happened to ahimsa?
Is it just for the birds and the bees?

What lips, what soles
swarmed across the river?
Is it hot on the other side?

Oh, so many questions, sir,
I cannot help myself
I cannot shut my mouth.

It's hard to hear you,
birds peck at sounds,
maggots gnaw since

even syllables have skin.
The kingdom of heaven
is tiny as a mustard seed

and you have crawled therein.
Mist pours from mango trees,
the moon soars in a sea of blood.

I see you at the rim of heaven
grown older still, bewildered, stooped,
dhoti flecked with drops of mud,

face seared by a moon
that has nothing
except its own inhuman glow,

the archipelago of light
afloat in monsoon air
where souls frail as pinpricks go.

Dear Mr. Gandhi
please talk to me now.
I am slow dancing

in the dark
with the untimely dead
and that is all I know.

FAISAL MOHYUDDIN

Faisal Mohyuddin, the son of immigrants from Pakistan, was born and raised in the Chicago suburbs. He has a BA in English from Carleton College and an MS in education from Northwestern University and is currently completing an MFA in fiction writing at Columbia College in Chicago. An excerpt from his novel-in-progress, *Muslimtown*, appeared in *MAKE: A Chicago Literary Magazine*. Other work has been published in *Poet Lore*, the *Atlanta Review*, *Free Lunch*, the *English Journal*, the *Flint Hills Review*, and *Hair Trigger*. He won first prize in the 2006 Ray Bradbury Creative Writing Contest, and his winning poem, "Eid-ul-Fitr, 1946," was featured on Chicago Public Radio's *848*. Mohyuddin teaches English at Highland Park High School. He and his wife live in Evanston, Illinois.

Being a Pakistani Punjabi Muslim Midwestern American has infused and confused my existence since 1978.

Ayodhya

After the Babri Masjid Massacre
Ayodhya, India—December 1992

Knowing you so well, Husham,
you must have been sitting at an old wooden desk,
hiding behind a wall of books, contemplating
the unifying potential of Rumi's poems
when the rioting suddenly broke, when the mobs flooded
the streets, heading straight towards the Babri—
that cursed house of God long evacuated
and left to crumble under the weight of the centuries.
That afternoon, children exiled into the bowels
of misunderstood history, suffering
from the inheritance of their parents' grievances,

hypnotized by stories that spoke of imaginary pasts,
of holy birthplaces and forgotten birthrights,
ripped through Ayodhya, roaring like a stampede
of elephants, thirsty for the taste of a brother's blood.
Convinced only a divine decree could inspire
so many to suddenly become so god-conscious,
even the most simple-minded onlookers
must have felt compelled to join in, to help dismantle
one version of history, brick by brick, limb by limb.
When darkness finally fell on our city, falling like a black veil,
as if trying to keep the stars from bearing witness
to this unholy event, from this suicidal December day,
the demolished edifice was mere backdrop.
The 3,000 corpses were what reminded us
that Ayodhya would belong to no one anymore.

Yet this city was still ours—
we grew up here, misfits who spent our days in the streets,
our nights sneaking off to the movie houses
to see our boy-dreams projected onto movie screens
as wide as the night. This is our Ayodhya.
Here we attended the same school our fathers did,
the one behind the dilapidated church, peopled by the poor
Hindu-converts who were fooled into believing
that Jesus was born blue—that the name
Krishna was rooted in the words Christ and Christian.
That was our Ayodhya. Do you remember
how we longed for school to end each afternoon,
suffering through the schoolmasters' thrashes,
generously intended to subdue our perpetual impatience?
We couldn't wait to go hide behind Black Joseph's
sweetmeat stand, positioned perfectly to steal quick glances
at the girls blossoming in our neighborhood.
Remember how boyishly we battled over Nargis,
the girl we renamed after the film goddess?
She taught us the meaning of lust

by occasionally winking at us with her dark eyes,
making us hard between the legs, an obvious embarrassment.
Do you remember how Black Joseph,
whenever he saw us eyeing Nargis, our crotches
pressed up against his stand, would sing songs stolen
from films—songs our fathers sang to us long
before we understood the meaning of heartache and loss
and memory? And how, lost in musical reveries,
Black Joseph, hands on hips, would whirl
like a drunk dervish, mocking us with his fluttering eyelashes?
How whenever he laughed he would be overcome
by a bout of coughing so violent he had to hold onto his
sarong-like dhoti to keep it from falling to his feet?

Husham, do you remember the sweet scent
of the mango trees on my uncle's farm in Amritsar,
their thick leaves dangling elegantly like earrings
from the ears of Queen Noor Jahan? Do you know
why we never went back there? Outside,
under their generous shade—in a darkness so viscous
it held us like a black net—we remained unaware
of the turbulence raging in my uncle's kitchen.
We never heard him cursing wildly, throwing guilt and history
in my father's face, who, I learned many years later,
had dared to bring a Muslim into a Brahmin home,
who threatened our family name with an unwashable stain.
My father—who always called your father *Bhaiya*
and taught me to call you by the same brotherly name—
never spoke back, allowed his brother-in-law
to beg Lord Krishna's blue face to curse my family
with sickness and a shameful legacy of barren daughters-in-law.
Protected from the sweltering summer sky
by the mango trees, we enjoyed our youthful ignorance,
counted the ants crawling up our legs,
and eventually admitted drowsiness, the heat heavy
on our eyelids, pushing them down, slowly until shut.

I leaned back in my charpoy, rested my head in my hands.
Between the dull thudding of ripe red mangoes
falling to the ground, I enjoyed the calming silence
of your sleep, and dreamed away the restlessness
I sometimes saw dancing in my mother's eyes.

My friend, it is a shame our mothers didn't talk more.
They both suffered from the same epidemic of silence,
a clinging to a nameless injury, one no words would heal,
one no amount of forgetting could ever undo.
I remember one Friday afternoon, when you disappeared
with your father into a masjid near the vacant Babri,
my mother asked that I come home to help her
chop greens for dinner. We were expecting company,
old family friends, people too important to disappoint,
and I was expected to be godlike, to sit silently in the corner
of the room, watchful, smiling, dead to the living.
After a morning of street cricket and wrestling
in the dusty school gardens, my face was dark with dirt,
and mud stained my clothes—I looked like a beggar,
absolutely shameful. My mother joked that I was too filthy
to be her son. As she washed my face, her hands
kneading at my skin, she let a long, deep sigh betray her smile.
When I asked her why her eyes looked so
all-of-a-sudden dim, her face became the sun,
no longer sad. She said she just preferred that I spend
more time indoors, out of reach of the sun's summer fury,
which—if I wasn't careful—would make me
dark-skinned forever, like an untouchable.

When your wife Jamila begged you to forget
Ayodhya, to find a teaching post in Lahore,
where Urdu's best writers spent their evenings
at the Pak Tea House—at least for your unborn children
if not for her—you pressed your body hard against hers
to still the violence of her breathing. You knew she had never felt

at home in India, had begged you since your wedding night
to do as her parents had done and migrate away
to Pakistan. But you refused to flee. You would not
tolerate her mistrust of Hindus, would not fall victim to a history
flooded with misinterpretations. In your eyes,
the mistake of Partition had disfigured the Subcontinent,
had left this land wounded, aching, fractured, forever searching
for wholeness. Now she curses your relentless optimism
and wishes to forget your ghost, which she sees forever
in your son's eyes. Bilal must be in school now, a small prince
of a boy who will soon inherit the poison of a mother's suffering.
Husham, when you were killed outside the Babri,
in the aftermath of the storm that bathed our city with blood,
each drop in the name of one god or another,
I fell against the wall, torn apart, mumbles of some broken language
spilling from my fumbling lips. With an aggression
that gave me nightmares for weeks, I seized the statues
my parents had given me, so placid and silent
on bookshelves and tabletops, no longer worthy
of my trust, and flung them to the floor.
Decapitated heads, amputated arms, severed legs flew
in all directions, in splashes of marble, stone, and porcelain.
My body quivered with the disease, I considered
prying out my eyes from my skull with my fingers,
but only pushed hard enough to see explosive red flares colliding
against the backs of my eyelids. Then I disappeared
to find you—*but all I saw were faces, glowing, alive with fury.*
Faces broken and blinking, without sequence, like film clips
sewn together haphazardly—faces lost in time, in slow-motion, overlapping,
becoming the same face. Faces white with fear, flowering
with a flourish of curses, some lips spewing spit, mixed with blood, dust.
Others stitched shut, with voices clogged in windpipes, the muffled sounds
of gagging and suffocation reverberating through the alleys.
I saw faces with eyes gouged out, limp optic nerves hanging flaccidly
from empty eye sockets. Faces singed, seared onto corpses,
strewn through the streets, left for the dogs to manage. Faces full
of tears, shame, happiness, disbelief. For a moment I saw

your face, one of the many—a transient flame, flickering, fading fast,
engulfed by even larger flames, consumed by chaos, disappearing
completely, drowned in a sea of other faces—forever lost, forever lost.

My dead brother, Ayodhya suffers without you,
continues to battle its own wounds, and I no longer know
what to believe in. The difficulty of Ghalib's poems
brought us together at school, while Amitabh Bachchan
united us in the evenings, in film. He was the hero of our lives,
defying the test of time with movie after movie,
handsome as ever, the only true actor-singer
Bollywood has ever known. His *Namak Halal* was our favorite,
with the crazy action sequences in which he would defeat
the weakling villains, each with a single punch.
We wanted to be him—or just like him
since we preferred to kiss the heroine at the end.
But such were the storyline formulas of Indian cinema—
nothing could ever be changed, and we knew
to let our dreams fill in the rest, to complete the vacancies
that perforated our lives. We were just two boys
too close to notice the differences that would fall between us
like worlds, two friends growing up, learning to absorb
the tremors of inheritance, the rhythmic pounding of
clashing histories, remaining unshaken, never questioning
the motherly silences that congealed in our memories,
that became stones and sunk into the sands of
our forgetting. Perhaps nothing has brought us so much
misery through the centuries than these religions,
these solemn ways of life and death and indifference.
And our abbreviated brotherhood was blessed to have
such perceptive fathers who shielded us from the foolishness
that accompanied blind faith, who taught us that new partitions
would not help us unravel our convoluted pasts.

Yes, Bhaiya, every year as a stranger I come to Ayodhya
under quiet circumstances—just the wind and me—
to keep myself from forgetting you. Yet I pray

for forgetfulness here, for some way to erase the events of
that bloody December, which replay themselves in my nightmares,
frame by frame. I have learned from the violence
that still stains our soil, that no one ever forgets
the things that must be forgotten. Forgetting, a kind of forgiveness,
eludes our people, keeps them helplessly bound to pain,
so easily ignited into bursts of hateful action.

Visiting you helps purge my despair, instills in me
a new kind of hope, one that propels me back
into my incomplete life in a faraway city. I have left Ayodhya
many times, and in leaving I continue to live.
This is a city still devoid of faith, a city wounded
and bleeding, a city once ours to trust, once ours to pass on.
I press my ears against your tombstone, flat on the ground,
closer to you. I feel its cold hardness and listen
for our fathers' songs to rise like phantoms from the earth.
From this fallen position I remember your voice,
remember how you impersonated Mohammad Rafi
with effortless precision, while I stretched to be Lata,
as we sang together the old songs. On the train home,
whenever my body begins convulsing in tremors of sadness,
these songs console my lostfulness and save me
from weeping loudly in the company of strangers.

Blood Harmonies

To remember my mother crouching in our kitchen,
putting into place a new floor of ceramic tiles,
is to remember her blood hopes, her effervescent hunger
to keep the feet of her five kids from slipping
into the wrong kind of slide. Stay one with one another,
in blood harmony, she would say, meaning
brother and sister, Muslim and Muslim, blood and blood.
Pointing down at the tiles, she would say,
Look how the pattern comes together,

forms a larger mosaic of meaning. You should live like this.
Most of the time, I nodded my head, not knowing
how else to respond, agreeing because it was simpler.
But sometimes, standing there, looking down
at a floor not yet finished, at naked patches revealing
a history of vinyl, broken and stained, I would think,
I just can't be happy living so small, so safe.
Then I would see, in those unfinished places, the face
of some girl I had met the other day,
whose name I never asked, knowing it was pointless . . .
I would stand there in the kitchen, thinking
how badly I wanted to know that girl's name, to believe in it
like a new religion, like my own blood,
how I wanted to let myself fall in love with her,
because that girl had smiled at me, because that girl was real
and alive, not like one of those phantom wives
my mother saw in her dreams and spoke of in metaphors.

Poem Inspired by a Note Found Scrawled onto the Inside Cover of *One Day at a Time in Al-Anon* Sitting on a Bookshelf at Café Ambrosia, Evanston, Illinois

> When my prince charming does come along
> I'll be down at the pond kissing frogs.

Perhaps it was because you woke up feeling lucky
that you laced up your nicest sneakers and went
hop-scotching to some frog-infested pond, armed
with your brightest shade of lipstick (red can turn on
even the most lackadaisical Joe—believe me, I know)
and an umbrella (in case it rains—or you discover
the need to beat sense into some idiot). Perhaps
you went there because you ran out of photos
to tear up and had grown tired of those same-old
Cure songs that made you feel less alone on bright

spring Sundays when you should be out with a fling
necking at some public park where joggers and
geriatrics can both cringe at the sight of two
amphibious tongues wrestling for a taste of home
in your mouths. Or perhaps, while perusing
dusty yearbooks at your kitchen table, reliving
forgotten memories, you suddenly remembered
the names of all the dorks you found hideous
back in high school and couldn't help but wonder,
as you gazed out at the bursts of pink in the trees,
how they had turned out, whether or not
those pimply faces might have metamorphosed
into something close to handsome. And perhaps
you are there now, at that pond, gazing down
into the muddy shallows, eyeing the frogs stationed
like guards, their bulging eyes peeking up
through the sticks and mossy scum, your lips puckered,
shaped like a flower, ready to kiss or be kissed.
Perhaps that's why you haven't answered, despite
how long I've waited, how hard I've knocked.

DILRUBA AHMED

Dilruba Ahmed's poems have appeared in *Blackbird, Born Magazine, Catamaran,* the *Crab Orchard Review,* the *Cream City Review, diode, Drunken Boat,* the *New England Review,* the *New Orleans Review,* and the *Asian Pacific American Journal.* Ahmed received first place for the *Florida Review's* 2006 Editors' Award and honorable mentions for the 2005 James Hearst Prize and the 2006 New Letters Award. She holds BPhil and MAT degrees from the University of Pittsburgh and an MFA from Warren Wilson College. Ahmed coedited *Going Public with Our Teaching: An Anthology of Practice* (Teachers College Press, 2005) while working as a project coordinator at the Carnegie Foundation for the Advancement of Teaching. She has given readings at the Bread Loaf Writers' Conference, Artwallah, and APAture. An educator for many years, Ahmed lives near Philadelphia.

> *A South Asian American with roots in Pennsylvania, Ohio, and Bangladesh, I've returned to Pennsylvania after eight years in the San Francisco Bay Area.*

The 18th Century Weavers of Muslin Whose Thumbs Were Chopped

after Agha Shahid Ali

They became extraneous.
By some brutal magic
those who spoke *ingrezi*
fashioned rice into cotton, made

slaves of them all.
                    Tonight
you're bewitched by a market
full of visions. Lit candles

wink and warn as rickshaws
approach, revealing pyramids
of oranges, drums of green
coconut, a man with pale
cabbages piled on top

of his head.
        What you've heard
of the weavers is no alchemy, it's true:
they could have woven
you a cloth as fine as pure mist.

Beyond silk. Beyond gossamer.
Twenty yards in a matchbox
like folded air. Or fifteen
through a golden band, diaphanous.

Later,
      will their stories vanish, too?
No traveler, no trader will recall
their wizardry among jute
rugs on the street, silken saris,

notched sugar cane, earthy
tea leaves that crumble—while absence
pulses like the phantom
thumbs. *Hush child, my eyes*
are so tired.
      Beyond the half-
glow of the city, a pond stagnates
full of plastic bags where someone
bathes his feet and dreams of

braiding his lover's hair.

Learning

We float through the stream,
past a woman whose aqua skirt flares
with every turn, past coiffed black hair

and powdered faces. A man with a
chunky silver belt buckle towers
over his partner. A loner dances solo

by the speakers an unchanging waltz.
Tonight we are learning to cha cha,
and you've finally conceded to learn

how to dance. We trip and we try,
and though our rhythm's not quite right,
we are full of drama like the woman

in the silver dress, tossing her head
at every turn. We hear only the drums,
the counting voice over speakers:

basic step, 1-2-3, breakaway—
and the fog clears, the mist that rolls
through the Santa Cruz mountains,

a specter or haunt, imperceptibly
surrounding us,
obscuring all that lies ahead:

a mountain darkened, a glittering
ocean, a stolid field of green. We join
the stream, the slow swirl of sheer

dresses and shining fabrics, trying
to keep our feet light, moving
but towards nothing, stumbling

and laughing, never changing partners
once. We break away—
and the headlines shout of baseball,

not bioterror, and Barry Bonds,
not bombings. We break away
from the gray teeth

of the buildings' remains, smoke rising
as though something has devoured
an enormous meal at the gritty scene.

Under the choke and snowfall
of dust, cardboard walls
cave in on our small worlds.

Never mind that *cha cha* means
uncle in Bengali. Never mind
that we don't have those leather-soled

dance shoes. I've worn my brown
silk blouse, the one I could never
wear when I taught first grade.

You've worn the navy cotton
oxford I bought four years ago.
Like invisible fish gulping

at the surface for air, we swim past
the folded bleachers in this makeshift
ballroom. The gymnasium echoes

of basketballs against backboards,
like small explosions
from the satellite's view. Here

no one knows our names,
but we know that this moment
of leaning and turning under the lights

will end, and we'll find ourselves
soon in the dark of the parking
lot: black sky and pavement,

black hair—yours and mine.
Black letters on the nameplate
outside my office door—must be

*a Muslim, a maniac, a terrorist
name.* I turn left and cross over,
bump into you, break our count,
and we start over, we try again.

Invitation

Join me at the dresser
where you sit in the dim photograph
folding your smooth black
hair into a bun, eyes darkened
with kajal, sari draped (is it blue?)
across one slim shoulder.

*But surely the heat will kill us.
Our bodies won't stand
the water, the sun.*

Walk stories with me
on the dirt path to the midnight
bazaar, where merchants
keep stalls open for Eid,
selling sparkly bangles
and milky-sweet *shondesh.*

On asthma days, breath comes
as though through a sieve.
The winter winds are full of dust.

We'll paddle across the silvery pond
where you swam daily as a child,
to the bamboo mat where your mother sits
in the photo, small arms
in her white sari, toothless smile against
my sister's acid-wash jean jacket.

In every newspaper,
the Dengue fever.
And my mother, gone.

Let's wander the orange halls
of your university, where you first began
the exchange of furtive love letters,
like the long cool drink
from the jug outside the classroom,
students squirming in the heat.

Now, an election year,
mobs rise in a cyclone's wave,
so much political unrest.

I want to sit with you
in the elegant symmetry
of the verandah,
the evening-cooled porch
filled with cousins, the mango tree
heavy with fruit.

The porch is boarded up now,
the house, long since divided
into smaller dwellings.

I thought you'd sail
into that sea
with me, into the water
that hangs at the horizon
like a pale slice
of slate.

So long since I stopped
sending crisp blue airmail.
And my mother, gone.

I knew so little of the distance
between Bryn Mawr
and Brahmanbaria, of Chillicothe
and Chittagong. I know
nothing of your hemisphere,
of your heartache.

How we climbed as children
to gather green coconut,
its sweet soft flesh.

Come: let's drive. We'll ride
the swells along the road
to the park, the bumps
next to trees whose roots
have been paved over
and are still gently pushing.

PRAMILA VENKATESWARAN

Pramila Venkateswaran is the author of *Thirtha* (Yuganta Press, 2002) and *Behind Dark Waters* (Plain View Press, 2008). She was a finalist for the Allen Ginsberg Poetry Award, and her work has appeared in journals in India, Canada, and the United States, including *Ariel, CALYX, Long Island Quarterly,* the *Nassau Review, Prairie Schooner,* and *Xanadu.* Born in Bombay, Venkateswaran immigrated to the United States in 1982 to pursue her doctoral degree in English at George Washington University. Her recent articles on global women's issues have appeared in *Women's Studies Quarterly* and in the anthology *Language Crossings: Negotiating the Self in a Multicultural World* (Teachers College Press, 2000). She teaches English and women's studies at Nassau Community College, New York.

A Tamilian Indian American living in New York, I write in English and translate modern Tamil poetry into English.

Draupadi's Dharma

How long is this war?
How much longer, Yudhisthira?
I want a normal life in Hastinapura,
in Mathura, somewhere.
I want you to be a normal husband,
your brothers to live normal lives.
I've forgotten what normal feels like
among carnage wrought by willfulness.

You talk of grand things,
like getting your kingdom back,
but what of your dharma toward me,
your Draupadi? And love?

Look around, dear Yudhisthira,
everywhere women yearn for the ordinary—
cook, clean, love, gossip, sleep—
dream ordinary dreams of years stretching out
like the view from a window,
trees against a blue sky, a road
with people beginning or ending their day,
birds pecking grain.

I want the simple,
the beginning when love created
the universe and the universe replied.
I do not want the poetry of incandescence,
exotic, grand truths, revelations.
I do not want to walk into a horizon lined
with fences of fire.

My spirit is resilient, no doubt,
despite my rape at that demon's wild hands,
your silence colder than death.
Listen, I'll be no scapegoat, no mute.
It's time to let go, Yudhisthira,
of your cock-eyed dharma;
I'm through.

Exile

Do you see, Fauzia? The sky is torn, letters bleed from it,
big, black letters stringing themselves into festoons,
weaving themselves around telephone cables, reaching
for flag poles, tall houses, trees, anything stately
that will make us look up with awe, as we are doing now,
pressing our fingers to our cheeks as words stencil the air
with indelible ink. Do you see what I see? The words,
one moment brilliant confetti scattering at a festival,

smudges the next, as if a bird has cut through the glyphs,
the old letters knocked off by newer ones, their brightness
piercing our eyes, forcing them shut. It's blazing,
but in halls within our eyes, streaked as if with henna,
we are unable to locate the familiar—the road climbing
up to the bridge and descending into the market place
with its fountains of voices . . . our briefcases, walking shoes,
diaries, that silk dress you gave me for my birthday,
even our men. Our men, Fauzia, look at them changing,
as the words dim and brighten with renewed force
and we shield our gaze so darkness veils our eyes
to keep them cool. I reach out to hold his hands
as I did when we first met at the café outside Kabul,
but they are old, damp wood that won't catch fire
however much I try to find fresh spots and hold to
them the light cupped in my numb fingers.
Our girls are in the porch with the heaviness of time
tethering their tongues, as letters from the wound
fasten themselves around their wrists and feet.
It's true, Fauzia, the words are now at eye level,
I know, despite my closed eyes and the twitching
nerves in your lids, I know the writing is growing
like ivy over buildings and valleys and around
our bodies. Our bodies, Fauzia, that have never felt
the prick of cords—except the needle for healing,
or the hurt of pleasure on the marriage bed—
now are held fast with bands and bracelets of threats.
Do you remember how we lay with abandon, eating
fried plantains on my grandmother's couch
opposite a framed picture of two Russian soldiers
in the mountains sitting by a fire lit by a peasant?
Is the sun still riding the mountain's edge?
Why is the house dark and where's everyone?
And, why don't I hear your voice, Fauzia?

BHARGAVI C. MANDAVA

Born in Hyderabad, India, Bhargavi C. Mandava grew up in New York City. Her fiction and poetry have appeared in such journals as the *Asian Pacific American Journal,* the *Konundrum Engine Literary Review,* and *Bangtale International,* and in the anthologies *Through a Child's Eyes: Poems and Stories about War* (Plain View Press, 2001), and *Another Way to Dance: Contemporary Poetry from Canada and the United States* (TSAR, 1996). She is the author of one novel, *Where the Oceans Meet* (Seal Press, 1996). In 1997, she received a Brody Arts Fund Fellowship in fiction. In 2006, Mandava was the curator of literature for Artwallah, the Festival of South Asian Arts in the Diaspora, and also worked on the Uncharted Storytelling Project. She is presently working on a short story collection and her next novel. She lives in Los Angeles.

My roots stretch from the Mandawa desert warriors of Rajasthan to the villages of Andhra Pradesh, over New York City and back to the California desert.

Of Starry Silence

When a chicken drinks water, it doesn't forget
to raise its head in thanks to god.
That's what his mother used to say as she
set food out on the table.

On the clay wall, the flickering candle lights
a photograph of his father and sister
who were shot down near the factory
where the workers stitch baseballs.

The island is overrun with bloodthirsty
leopards lurking in the sugar cane, leaping
at children, said his mother. So with blessings
of Legba and St. Catherine, he began rowing.

With each stroke, a farewell memory:
hot wax falling on painted calabashes;
frangipani blossoms at the Iron Market;
neroli and vetiver; squeezing into camions.

Back in Raboteau, children continued
to play by chasing off pigs and dogs
digging up shallow graves. All this,
in between bites of mango and breadfruit.

At 4 am, the church bells ring in Port-au-Prince.
At 6 am, a jogger on the Miami coast finds
his 15-year-old body, stiff like an iguana
from swallowing half an ocean.

He's facedown; the white sand clings to his cheeks
as a policeman raises his head and turns him over.
From out of his damp denim pocket, fall black dice
showing a pair of ones like two fallen stars.

Moonsweets

The guava tree shimmers
as a parrot cleans its green face.
Ammamma stares straight ahead
as if rudraksha beads were passing
beneath her thumb, but
she is not meditating—
she is cooking.
Once, the scent of sesame and
brown sugar on her fingers
from rolling sweet butterballs
smelled of jasmine buds too.
She does not wear flowers in her hair
since her husband died.

It is a breezy afternoon sounding of
rickshaw bells and wet saris
striking laundry stones.
Her granddaughter scampers down
the garden walkway, screaming news.
Her small, perfect fingers tuck
a hibiscus blossom behind
her Ammamma's ear.
The woman looks at herself rippling
in the cask of dark water,
amidst fallen leaves and mosquitoes.
"I'm hungry," says the girl
because she is growing,
so Ammamma shakes out her hands and
wipes them on her widow-white sari.
Through the gauze and sun, her arms and
feet seem to disappear; she is half ghost.
As she walks to the cupboard, the
hibiscus slips, leaving a comet-trail
of vermillion down her back.
Her granddaughter does not notice
as she eyes the silver canister
brimming with pale full moons.

REENA NARAYAN

Reena Narayan was born in the Fiji Islands and immigrated to California in the early 1970s. She received her BA and MA in English literature from California State University, Fullerton. Narayan's work appears (under her previous name of Reena Sharma) in anthologies such as *Contours of the Heart* (Temple University Press, 1998) and *Desilicious* (Arsenal Pulp Press, 2004), as well as in *India Currents Magazine*. Narayan's short stories have been featured at Artwallah, the Festival of South Asian Arts in the Diaspora. She is currently working as a fourth-grade teacher in the city of La Puente, where she resides with her husband and two daughters.

> *As a child new to America, I knew one English word . . . that one sweet, brown word the color of my skin, transcending every linguistic barrier known to children. Choc-lit.*

My Daughter

You stand beneath an umbrella-less sky
face lifted like a sunflower to the clouds
hands perched against five-year-old hips in
a dress the color of oceans
waiting for rain.

You ask me questions I do not have answers to
like does God live in raindrops
and how did it all begin
trees, cats, turtles, bugs,
dinosaurs, chocolate bars, babies,
everyone and everything

questions I have stopped asking.

You do not have that Indian woman heaviness
this lump in our breasts

that is beyond cancer
beyond biology;
we pass it on
mother to daughter to daughter
a silent heirloom.

We do not ask questions
for fear of living in doubt
or being told
we talk too much.
We drown inside
caught within those quiet spaces
buried beneath our footsteps,
between loss and acceptance,
formality and desire.
We make holy offerings
coconuts, marigolds,
silver-foiled sweets
praying for our children,
our husbands,
our parents, forgetting
ourselves.

It is different with you
you are Dora the Explorer
off to a new adventure, my daughter
in pink plastic boots and a bracelet of hearts
hair unbraided, light as a molecule
you will jump in puddles and get your dress wet
you will ask howcome-why questions
even if there are no answers
you will stand in the rain
with your mouth open, so sure
that if you swallow one drop
you will know
everything.

Tobacco Wrapped in *The Fiji Times*

My grandmother sits
in her wheelchair
wearing polyester pants and striped ankle socks
smoking a newly rolled cigar.

It was sent from overseas via
a relative's suitcase along with six
pieces of coconut candy and a jar
of star fruit pickles,
her treasures tucked between pages of
The Fiji Times.

Just one puff, she says, even though
she's already had a stroke
and knows better,
her eyes glint with mischief.

How can I say no,
she reasons during her third inhale,
*when Bharat sent it all the way from Suva
just for me,*
her heart is alive with the joy
of being remembered
by someone so far away.

*He knew I always enjoyed a good cigar
an old woman like me,* she chuckles,
the smoke spirals above our heads
like airy ghosts
don't tell your mother.

I stare at the wheels of her chair
and her immovable legs
drawn together like a child, she
has not walked these three years.

She hands me the missing pages
of a September newspaper
Bharat used as a gift wrap
creased with wrinkles and smelling of leaves
and spices that have traveled over oceans
read me what is going on back home
Then she pushes herself forward
to hear better, her shoeless feet
turned inwards.

A month after her stroke
she gave away all her saris
silks the color of pomegranate seeds
and peacock feathers
some never worn still smelling
of mothballs and cloves
A wheelchair was not made for an Indian woman,
she announced, adjusting and readjusting,
shifting and rolling, wearing
pants like a man.

The tobacco's smoke
rises in the air,
I unravel the newspaper
brown flecks rain in my lap
as I scan headlines about Fiji's
Labor Party and two men on trial
for treason
and a fire in a Lautoka building.

Did anyone die?
she wants to know.

I turn to the next page
past sports and entertainment
to the obituary section

photographs of the dead
with serious camera eyes and half smiles
once-in-a-lifetime studio portraits.

Read me their names.

She leans even closer
her hair the scent of coconut oil
her eyeblinks
reminding me of a
blackbird perched on a branch
eager for the familiar
for any news from home.

I read slowly:
Ram Nand
Ashlini Singh
Ram Rati Sharma.

I look to see if she recognizes any of the names,
but she is quiet
I continue:
Mahendar Tulsi
Sukhraj Maharaj
Bindar Prasad.

Do you know any of them? I finally ask
and she smiles leaning back,
When you live in a small, small place for so long,
everyone is your relative,
one way or another.

She takes another puff,
her tobacco
laced with nostalgia
and the memory of those gone and

those still living
so far away.

The end of her cigar burns
like tiny afternoon suns
I am dazzled by this ancient dance
between smoke and light.

I give her back the newspaper
and she folds it in her lap
like an old wedding sari
careful not to let it snag
or rip inside its softness.

HOMRAJ ACHARYA

Homraj Acharya grew up in southern Nepal. A graduate of the University of Colorado at Boulder and American University, his publications in Nepali include a novel, *Nirdosh Kaidi* (Bhimshira, 1995), two collections of poetry, *Jeevit Kankal* (Unnayan, 1999) and *Alubarima Deuta* (Kalchahra, 2003), and one translation, *The Principal's Secret* (Ratan Puslak Bandar, 1997). His writing in English has been published in *Salt Hill, Wind,* the *Kathmandu Post, Strategic Confusion,* and *Walkabout.* He is now a public policy analyst in Washington, D.C., working on education issues, and an activist for democracy and social justice. He founded the grassroots nonprofit Books in Every Home.

> *I am a rural Nepali and an urban Washingtonian, with a buffalo-riding past and a Metro-riding present.*

The Silk-Cotton Tree

These are the monsters, as wide and difficult
and towering as the universe.
Listen. It's different from yours, of course.

It's a city, cut and crossed by the cracks of bark,
and beetles live on these thoroughfares
with red wings, the color of fecundity and anger.
In their sweet shops the bees are armed,
and the vultures on top of it all
coating the leaves with a brown waste
that looks precisely like ice cream.
Everyone is hungry.
You never know what your neighbors will do.

It's a watchtower for thieves.
You climb on it to look for jackals
who might covet your goats,
to hunt for tigers, foxes, pretty girls

on the riverbank where if you're quick
you can steal their clothes as they bathe
like the god Krishna as a naughty boy.
Those religious stories can give you good ideas.

It's a cup of milk.
You feed its flowers to your water buffalo,
and also the saplings.

It's a bed.
There are pods to be cracked,
and within them whorls of fluff
to stuff into mattresses and pillows,
the carrier of the life of the tree, the cotton seeds,
in each pod there are hundreds, tasting like sunflower seeds.
It's said that a pillow made of silk cotton
will talk to you at night.

It's a party,
candle wax hanging from its leaves.
You can slice up the abandoned hives
and melt them on the fire into brown holiday candles.

It's the fire itself.
The heart is made into matchsticks,
the limbs thrown into the hearth
to heat the milk,
to heat the stolen honey,
to heat the bee larvae that taste like eggs.

It's a red-light zone. High up the vultures copulate
with screams of excitement.
On the fat triangles where branches meet
boys play music, dreaming of legends.
Below in the underbrush a girl and boy come together
like a flute with the lips of Krishna.

It's a billboard for names and dates,
Red Cunt, Rattling Balls,
Fuck Fuck Fucking
Bhim Fucked Draupadi.

Each tree has a name.
The Pillar. The Umbrella.
Goblin, Snaky, Holey, Crooked One,
Father Burial.
The roots are so big they must have spirits,
they must be a palace for the naga snakes.

Where the trunk meets the ground
there is a hollow sprinkled with holy water,
marigolds, bel leaves.
A goat is sacrificed, one of the goats the tigers didn't get
or the goddess Durga at the time of brown holiday candles.
Leaves are mixed with cowdung to fertilize the fields,
and there is rice.
It's a shrine, it's rain, it's a new year.

The Kerosene Stove

The kerosene stove has no home.
Monday by the water bucket, Tuesday by the leg of the bed,
sometimes greeted by the hand, sometimes by the foot,
its face kissing the burnt bottoms of skillets,
aluminum saucepans, kettles, pressure cookers.
It is really unfortunate. It had bad karma to be married to this house.
It was a dowry, now it nestles
by rice sacks in the corner, or underneath the bed that squeaks
like the mice in the ceiling
so that neighbors know the whole world about you,
but hey, who cares what they think?
The rice sack is hungry, its belly empty.

Potatoes complain, tomatoes moan,
there are the usual cracks from the bitter gourds.

A black and white TV flickers in the evening.
The Nepalese delegation to the United Nations
voted its approval of the American proposal.
The Crown Prince has felicitated the soccer team
upon its departure for the Asian games.
Her Royal Highness has felicitated
an organization that teaches women to knit.
In the day a radio made in China sings about love.

The cups are steel,
they'd burn the fingers of the unaccustomed,
but anyway tea has to be served and the housewife
is a good finance minister for such a nation,
these steel cups are her credentials.
She's a good friend of the stove,
it fattened him for his B.A., B.Ed., M.A.,
certificate from the Kwality Computer Institute,
certificate from the Fluorescent Language Institute,
M.Ed., LLB, a lawyer,
a lecturer in socioeconomics and anthropology
from 6 a.m. to 8 a.m. at the campus and
from 9 a.m. to 5 p.m. a teacher of English
at the Celestial Stars Secondary School.
He teaches, he writes, he attends conferences
but mosquitoes, those mosquitoes don't give a damn about his bigness.
And as for the river,
the fetid microbial juice of the garment factory,
juice of the distillery, molasses of sewage,
the sugar cane pulp of a million stomachs,
it doesn't respect him, it just likes his nose.

What about the *Gorkhapatra,* the *Kantipur,* the *Kathmandu Post?*
The eyes first want to eat the ads. Any new schools?

The ads tease you, let you down. Your friend
is the stove, it was there before any of the jobs, its smell
has seeped into the linoleum, the concrete floor
of this room and the last one too.
What is a job anyway? Pushing the sun
down the hill every day, that's what they say.
That's what they do, the big guys, displace a thousand suns,
a thousand stoves, every day more sugar cane pulp.
But as for us, the rest of us,
bigness never rises above the surface of the paper.

R. PARTHASARATHY

R. Parthasarathy is the author of *Rough Passage* (Oxford University Press, 1985), a long poem, and editor of *Ten Twentieth-Century Indian Poets* (Oxford University Press, 2002). His work has appeared in the *Times Literary Supplement, Poetry,* the *Norton Anthology of World Masterpieces,* and *Penguin New Writing in India.* Parthasarathy's translation of the fifth-century Tamil epic *The Tale of an Anklet* (Columbia University Press, 1993) received several awards, including the 1995 Indian National Academy of Letters Translation Prize and the 1996 Association for Asian Studies Ramanujan Book Prize. Educated in India, England, and the United States, he spent several years as a literary editor with Oxford University Press, New Delhi, and was a member of the University of Iowa's International Writing Program. Three of his manuscripts are currently under consideration by publishers: *A House Divided* (poems), *The Earliest Tamil Poems* (translations), and *One Hundred Poems from the Sanskrit* (translations). Parthasarathy is a professor emeritus of English and Asian studies at Skidmore College in Saratoga Springs, New York.

> *I was born in Tamil Nadu, India, and grew up in Mumbai (Bombay).*
> *I translate poetry from Tamil, Sanskrit, Hindi, and Urdu.*

from *Exile*

3

It was always evening when we entered
a city. Empty streets,
perhaps a drizzle or, as in Asia,

dust and famished children stopped us.
We had grown accustomed
to the city walls in Istanbul and Jerusalem.

Deserts in Syria and Iran. Once,
we passed a caravanserai, Bedouin huts,
qanats (more marvelous than the Pyramids),

rivers, soldiers. Boats waited
in the harbor. In the distance,
Samothrace, barely visible.

And our bodies in the sand,
as a full moon teased the Aegean.
Across the seas a new knowledge,

sudden and unobtrusive as first snow
transforming the landscape,
rinses speech, affirms the brown skin

and the heart beating to a different rhythm.
("*Querido,*" she had said, "whatever common things
our love fed on you have changed.")

The streets are noisy, and trees
on Malabar Hill blind with dust.
Spring had gone unnoticed

except for the fountains of color in the park.
Like a hand at rest, the pelagic city
is immobile. Between us there is no commerce.

4

Cleansed, the ash of old cities
(curled up and ochred at the edges
now, in the photograph)

hot under my feet, I return
to the city I had quarreled with,
a euphoric archipelago,

to the hard embrace of its streets,
its traffic of regulated
affections, uneventful but welcome.

5

The city reels under the heavy load
of smoke. Its rickety legs break
wind, pneumatically of course,

in the press of traffic.
The sun burns to cigarette ash.
Clouds hiccough, burp

from too much fume. Birds, too,
struggle, pressing thin feathers
against the glass of air.

I am through with the city.
No better than ghettos, the suburbs.
There, language is a noise,

and streets unwind like cobras
from a basket. A cow stands
in the middle combing the traffic.

A cloud unfurls, scarfs in the evening.
I loosen the knot in my throat,
and set off towards the sea.

The last sun comes hurtling at me.
Sand turns gold in my hand.
Boats squiggle on the water.

Cautiously masts sniff at the wind,
wipe off the odor
of land with clean sails.

6

Gulls wrinkle the air.
The boat heaves, opens the river's eye
in the twinkling of a street.

The engine stops.
Houses drop into place. From the funnel
smoke balloons towards Ilhas.

I step out, and a *carreira*
takes me to the heart of Goa.
Echo of immaculate bells from hilltops

flagged with pale crosses.
Under the sun's oppressive glare
he* stands alone

in a corner, an unrepentant schoolboy,
book in hand,
spanning an empire

from the Tagus to the China Sea.
I stop to take a picture:
a storm of churches breaks about my eyes.

7

It's a tired sea that accosts the visitor
between Fort St. George and San Thome.
Here, once, ships bottled the harbor

with spices, cinnamon, and cloves.
Inland, an old civilization
hissed in the alleys and wells.

---

*Camões, the Portuguese poet, whose statue in Old Goa is surrounded by the Sé Cathedral, the
Basilica of Bom Jesus, and the Churches of St. John of God and Our Lady of Rosary.

The sun has done its worst:
skimmed a language,
worn it to a shadow.

The eyes ache from feeding too much
on the ripe fruits of temples.
Bridges tame unruly rivers.

The hourglass of the Tamil mind
is replaced by the exact chronometer
of Europe. Now,

cardboard-and-paper goddesses (naturally
high-breasted) look down on Mount Road.
There is no fight left in the old beast.

Time has plucked her teeth. Francis Day
has seen to that. What have I come
here for from a thousand miles?

The sky is no different.
Beggars are the same everywhere. The clubs
are there, complete with bars and golflinks.

The impact of the West on India
is still talked about,
though the wogs have taken over.

The Concise Kamasutra

Under the warm coverlet my woman sleeps on.
I am drenched in the intractable scent of her hair:
the notion has often crossed my mind—
I should crumple it up like a handkerchief
that I could press to my face from time to time.
Meanwhile wakeful hands peel the skin off the night;

I drink from her tongue in the dark.
Our breaths tip the room over to one side:
the tight hardwood floor groans
under the slew of discarded clothes.
We shut the whole untidy threadbare world out—
dogs, telephones, and the thin indifferent rain.

Remembered Village

If you love your country, he said, *why are you here?*
Say, you are tired of hearing about
all that wonder-that-was-India crap.
It is tea that's gone cold: time to brew a fresh pot.

But what wouldn't you give for one or two places in it?
Aunt's house near Kulittalai, for instance.
It often gets its feet wet in the river,
and coils of rain hiss and slither on the roof.
Even the well boils over.
Her twelve-house lane is bloated with the full moon,
and bamboos tie up the eerie riverfront
with a knot of toads.

A Black Pillaiyar temple squats at one end of the village—
stone drum that is beaten thin on festivals by the devout.
Bells curl their lips at the priest's rustic Sanskrit.
Outside, pariah dogs kick up an incense of howls.

And beyond the paddy fields,
dead on time, the Erode Mail rumbles past,
a light needle of smoke threading remote villages
such as yours that are routinely dropped by schedules,
and no trains are ever missed.

PURVI SHAH

Purvi Shah's poetry has appeared in *Borderlands: Texas Poetry Review,* the *Brooklyn Review, Many Mountains Moving,* the *Massachusetts Review, Meridians,* and the anthology *Contours of the Heart: South Asians Map North America* (Asian American Writers' Workshop, 1996). Her first book of poems, *Terrain Tracks* (New Rivers Press, 2006), won the Many Voices Project prize. Shah is a former poetry editor of the *Asian Pacific American Journal.* She holds an MA in American literature from Rutgers University and is the recipient of a Virginia Voss Poetry Award from the University of Michigan. Born in Ahmedabad, India, Shah lives in New York City, where she recently served for more than seven years as the executive director at Sakhi for South Asian Women, a community-based anti–domestic violence organization. She is currently traveling, consulting on the issue of violence against women, and working on a second collection of poetry.

> *Purvi Shah is a New Yorker with a Southern heart due to her time in Georgia and Virginia. Here's to the Braves and to Southern charm with Northern attitude!*

Made in India, Immigrant Song #3

(a note from a New York City streetwalker)

Some worker in the sweat
of Madras, some former weaver
from Kashmir, some hand in Ahmadabad's dust,
has been pounding iron again.

The New York City streets swell with feet;
multihued tracks glide over the flat steel
disks which offer entry into the city's interior
lairs. The writing seeps through our soles
though few fathom the signature, "Made
in India." These alien

metal coins, transported
like my birth, mask
a labyrinth of tunnels
in a city where origin
and destination are confused.
Sometimes I wear the stamp
on myself; sometimes I feel
the wear of a surrounding world erase
the fine etchings. Here the imprint

of India is a traveler's
mutation: the body's chamber is made
hole, the skin not smooth, circular,
but cloaking a bumpy network
of channels, spirit mobile, expanding.

Unhoming

Before you beheld the moon, you would see
          shadow—a homeless dog running without pack across
                    street, a cat shivering along sidewalks your hand counts.
This end of the street to that end. Somehow in this moving lives,

you had returned to another same
block. The streets here, no surprise. Night
approached: your misgivings awoke.

In the day, the house would go about
its business, this sequence of cleaning, making
food, slapping clothes, making food, disrobing
          the line, making food, exhausted head

searching for a semi-flat pillow, the body at last   unrolling.

In day, you wifed. You create clink of cups, release comfort to *comfort*.
On a dust-scarred porch, you thrust the unraveling broom into

the beyond, scattering pigeons, straying the cat, shooing
dogs yearning to domicile. You strode from the baring

of teeth, the possible punctures, the vertigo between
your ears. This vision curls your toes at night, as the moon
unveils your quieted fear—to never cross dust, trail the untraced,

taskless except for journey itself.

Nature's Acre
POSTED

Here the roads are newly christened with names:
anonymous slab of asphalt sedimented into a label.
Every seventy-seventh tree is branded
with an echo of conversation: cattlery, no hunting,
Route 804. There is grass the orange of rusted

barnacle, a vintage migrated from some crazy
Italian painter who couldn't replicate
the color of fire & so doused her brush wet
with cerulean into the flames. Blades

of purple fence against the green, interlocking
into a barb wire entry at nature's neck. There are no factories, no gray
    smoke cracking
the air, but there is a red Taurus creeping
through the hills. There are no canned markets, preserved,

yet W. J. Carpenter's Chicken Coop &
Crafts stakes a claim from 1888 for the fresh
kill, a live wire framing the grain encircled
into a silo, a pitcher of concrete pottery, stoneware
for a sweet evening meal. There is a calf nestling in the wheat trough,
a mother who nibbles on the plump cheeks. The Mountain View
Italian Kitchen rests next to a clan of graves, peace jutting. A train

that crawls with a Louis Armstrong rumble through
the mist—a cycloptic eye diffracting dust and danger. Air
minted green every exhale. Within the knell
of it all, mountains, hills,
mountains, mountains, hills.

KAZIM ALI

Kazim Ali is the author of two books of poetry, *The Far Mosque* (Alice James Books, 2005), winner of Alice James Books' New England/New York Award, and *The Fortieth Day* (BOA Editions, 2008). He is also the author of the novel *Quinn's Passage* (blazeVox books, 2005), named one of "The Best Books of 2005" by *Chronogram* magazine, *The Disappearance of Seth* (Etruscan Press, 2009), and *Bright Felon: Autobiography and Cities* (Wesleyan University Press, 2009). His work has been featured in *Best American Poetry 2007*, the *American Poetry Review*, the *Boston Review*, *Barrow Street*, *jubilat*, and the *Massachusetts Review*. He teaches at Oberlin College and the University of Southern Maine's Stonecoast MFA program. He is a founding editor of Nightboat Books.

> *Of Egyptian, Iraqi, and Iranian descent, my family has lived in Tamil Nadu since the eighteenth century and during Partition scattered to Andhra Pradesh and Karachi.*

The River's Address

Slow in the evening light through tree-covered streets
sounds develop unenvelopable—

Troubador, river-citizen, can you navigate the sound's course
to my far shore's ecstasy?

Be gray here, be broken and strafed, fully roused and drawn here,
like a compass needle, find yourself bound and unintelligible.

You followed the shrift north from the city into the mountains,
to the place you eddy, churn, spell out the moon's tidal courses.

River-chaser, compass-worn, here the source spills to the sea,
and here the waters wend from the sea back to the source.

Unsire yourself—instead of street-maps and sounding depths
trace your name, trace the trees, trace the night into your mind.

Close your eyes and listen to the sound—try to remember—
or try to forget—here is the place you could turn and return.

Thicket

The story unfolds like this: a blameless father
loves the as yet unharmed son.

The son is somewhat randy and alarmed
at his appearance in an orthodox world.

Does it hurt him that he's been cut from the tribe of sons
who believe, are unarmed, who recite all the rules?

It's the father believes in God.
The son believes in the father.

The father in this story is guileless,
not trying to call God's bluff.

And unbelievably to all,
the son willingly opens his throat to the universe.

Neither one of them seeking to see Him,
not saying His name, not asking to be saved.

Event

Eight white birds, wings tipped with black, flying away. Snow stretches
below from dark to darkness.

*This is the image of the soul leaving, says Catherine. I sent this postcard to my
friends to announce the death of my sister.*

Dusty blue above the pyramid of Saqqara. The kingdom ends here and the desert begins.

Near a carved doorway, a guard lurks. For five pounds he lets me go down into the cold inner tombs.

There, the ancient etchings have been defaced by hieroglyphic graffiti. "First Dynasty ruffians," the guard explains, in pieces.

The roof is missing from the temple at the gate. Only the pillars attest to it.

There is a consonant in the middle of my Arabic name that my tongue cannot manage.

I mispronounce myself.

In a room full of shards at the museum, realizing the Egyptian artists *practiced.* Over and over again: a human figure from the side. Two feet evenly placed.

No attempt at approaching or retreating figures.

I love this painting of the cathedral by Van Gogh, says Catherine. *There is no door, no way to get in.*

MONICA FERRELL

Monica Ferrell's first poetry collection, *Beasts for the Chase* (Sarabande, 2008), won the Kathryn A. Morton Prize in Poetry. Her poems have appeared in journals such as the *Boston Review*, the *Nation*, the *New York Review of Books*, the *Paris Review*, and *Tin House*. She is also the author of the novel *The Answer Is Always Yes* (The Dial Press/Random House, 2008), which was a Borders Original Voices Selection and named among Booklist's Top Ten Debut Novels of 2008. A former Wallace Stegner Fellow and "Discovery"/*The Nation* prizewinner, she is an assistant professor in the creative writing program at Purchase College and lives in Brooklyn.

> *The daughter of an Indian woman and a white American man from the South, Monica was born in New Delhi and raised just outside New York City.*

Confessions of Beatrice D'Este

When you consider all I have left behind,
The ermine ruffs, glasses that sang out like sirens
At a finger's tap, silver fish traveling
Upon gilt plates like ruptured silk or mercury,
When you recall my long afternoons, sunlight
Trailing along the floor like heavy velvet,
My pearl-crusted carriage, jester, my guitar,

What should I miss? Remember, I was also a mother,
Two sea-horses once swam out from my ocean.
I was even devoted. I hovered like a cloud
At the cribs' edge, watching their limbs grow tight.
Day after day, my white face played parasol
Sheltering those saplings and the fantastic dreams
Assembling on their bodies' trunks like greenery.

And yet only dregs of that elixir stain my glass,
All that has all faded, gone from me in heat;
Now I wonder: what were they truly, so young
They could not return the river of my love
But a couple of trembling puppies, blindly licking?
Though I shall always wish them well, I have washed
My hands of such salt. The thing I miss came earlier.

Listen, when the doctors finally carried me
Wrapped in linen and sprinkled with camphor,
I saw a scene frescoed on my eyelids' vellum
I hadn't imagined for years. I thought I'd lost
That errant gem, yet like the oyster
Found it neatly pearled within when my hinge
Flew open in death. It's simple, really:

The first night my lord laid me down in our bed
He slit me wide as a flower's green calyx.
Then, bending back my branches for grafting,
Skillfully he pinned me. Later he blessed my hands
And kissed my lips like departing snowflakes
Before falling back on his pillow, a monument
Of impassive sandstone I knew to leave alone.

Watching him snore, at first I felt hurt
But then a girlish filament of fire
Made my whole body flame. Do you see?
Lying there in the sheets, my body beaten
Thinner than gold leaf, I had become bodiless
Vapor, a musical note, a vanishing point or door:
He had used me so completely I was seen through.

The Coin of Your Country

When I take my scissors to your shirts,
I am frightened: not that they will whimper

But that they won't understand the violence I mean.
That kind of violence is the other side of love,

Bright as a light-saber and permanent
As the angel's swords above Eden
Barring that couple with a final X,
That violence means a love strong as death.

Once *Sie ist mein leben,* you said, meaning me
And I took those words personally
And knocked upon the door of my heart
Until all its birds flooded to you, in a rush—

Like the Iroquois, I tugged on our peace-pipe,
I wrote your name in smoke. Then went home
With my pockets rolling in shining glass beads,
My pockets so rich with the coin of your country.

In the Binary Alleys of the Lion's Virus

Sorrento, your sun is light yellow lemonskin, your sky
Purling out like a farther surf on which I ride away
From that secret in a German town. I left behind
A dragon of enigma to fester there without me, I left
A small god ticking like a time bomb: a tiny jade statue suspended
By magnets in the vulva of a prehistoric temple. Here
In the oyster of your mornings I wake as lead.
                                        Once I was a knight
Who rode out in search of grail, now I am just a husk
Of armor with the grey squid of memory inside—I have forgotten
Land and tongue, I have forgotten everyone. Only I see
An emblem, some kind of lion arrant on ash-argent ground
A creature I greeted once in a dream: yes, at the crossroads of the hallowed
    grove
He kissed me—and must have slipped this curse between my lips.

Love, the Kunstkammer Version

after Peter the Great's collection of fetal oddities

With just the indentation of a line
Where an eye should have come to the fore
And an impress, an inch-length wrinkle
For his unopening mouth, near by pinpricks
Which dictate in faint constellations whiskers
That never formed—seed-points, God's dots
Left unconnected on such paper—the world's
Smallest white dog sits gamely in his glass cage,
Closed off by its dark fluid from all change
Like Laika left trailing in space, that moon room
Where everything is backward, broken, erased
As bridges lifted on the Neva, your diffident
Silence to my last letter, or that breath which stops
My saying what swims me too, unhurt and whole.

RAVI SHANKAR

An associate professor and the poet-in-residence at Central Connecticut State University, Ravi Shankar is the founding editor of the international online journal of the arts *Drunken Boat*. His book of poems, *Instrumentality* (Cherry Grove, 2004), was named as a finalist for the 2005 Connecticut Book Awards, and his creative and critical work has appeared in such publications as the *Paris Review, Fulcrum, McSweeney's,* the *AWP Writer's Chronicle,* and *Scribner's Best American Erotic Poems from 1800 to the Present,* among others. Shankar is the coeditor of *Language for a New Century: Contemporary Poetry from Asia, the Middle East and Beyond* (W. W. Norton, 2008) and has received a Summer Literary Seminars fellowship to Kenya and the Connecticut Commission on Culture & Tourism's FY09 Fellowship in Poetry. He has two poetry chapbooks forthcoming in 2010.

> *A Chennai and Coimbatore Tamilian from Northern Virginia, as apt*
> *to say bugging as romba nandri, I identify with language's musical*
> *inflections, rather than a particular race or nation.*

The Flock's Reply to the Passionate Shepherd

After Christopher Marlowe

Marooned upon this grassy knoll,
We wander lost from vale to pole,
Our wooly backs resemble thorn,
It's been a while since we've been shorn.

You waste your time trying to woo
That nymph who never will see you.
Since it's shepherd that you are,
You're better off courting a star.

But over here, your loyal flock
Needs no clasp, no precious rock
To follow you from field to field:
If love's your need, we can but yield.

Have you not heard us cry and bleat
When you approach us, then retreat?
We miss your orders and your laugh,
We even miss your clouting staff.

Save those gowns made of our wool,
No need to make belts or to pull
Posies from the hillside's crease—
That nymph is what we call a tease.

Just as the hours wing away,
There are some sheep that love to play:
If such delights your mind might move
Then live with us and be our love.

Before Sunrise, San Francisco

Bruno's by candlelight,
The jacketed barkeep counting
Tips from a jam jar and horseshoe
Booths burnished a bit too bright,

Yet the stained mahogany walls
And the lazy lament of Spanish
Horns from speakers huddled
In the corner speak a different

Language altogether, one that rolls
Effortlessly off the tongue and fills
The room like myrrh, a promise sent
That four walls can indeed keep out

The world, that when horns wail
For percussion and those walls
Are elegantly attired, why there
Is no need to ponder the gristle

In the Mission outside, no need
To wonder why that one left you
Or why you are always too
Late. The weight of your existence

Roughly equals the martini glass
In front of you, the thick mass
Of the past collapses into brightness
As well-lit as the dripping star.

At the center of your table.
Nod. Snap your fingers. Order
Another drink. Let horns grieve,
Let the wristwatch think on sheep

Before you leave. Tonight,
The only eyes on you are two
Pimentos stuffed into olives
Bloated with vermouth and gin.

Return to Mumbai

Bombay no longer, the island
Circumscribed by water exhausts
Herself in rain. For six months,

Her suitors, Vasai, Ulhas, Thane,
Spar, each swelling, vigorously
Surging, empurpling against

The horizon's taut washboard.
She, placid, stares breathless,
Smiles the smile of a schoolgirl

Whose step-father has just left
For London and decidedly opens
To each. Already, her soil soaks.

Already, she sings in preparation,
Rust-colored flames smoldering
Compost, plastic tarps flapping,

Held down by planks, stones,
Discarded tires; dirt roads gravid
With rickshaws, vegetable wallahs

Whipping bullocks, Tata trucks
Distended with diesel, yellow
And black taxis like so many drones

Evacuating the hive, bicycles,
Ambassadors, Maruti Suzukis,
Creaking double decker buses

Emblazoned with the latest
Bollywood star, women in fraying
Saris, barefoot men collecting

Alms, children praying, their shape
More rail than real. From an island
Mother, rising water fathers

This mitotic *bharathanatyam,*
An embryonic dance held
Until the obstetrician's arrival.

VINAY DHARWADKER

Born in Pune, India, Vinay Dharwadker was educated at Delhi University and the University of Chicago. He is the author of two collections of poems, *Sunday at the Lodi Gardens* (Viking, 1994), and *Someone Else's Paradise* (Viking, forthcoming). His editorial projects include *The Oxford Anthology of Modern Indian Poetry* (1995), *The Collected Poems of A. K. Ramanujan* (Oxford University Press, 1995), *The Collected Essays of A. K. Ramanujan* (Oxford University Press, 1999), and *Cosmopolitan Geographies: New Locations in Literature and Culture* (Routledge, 2001). A translator of modern Hindi, Marathi, Urdu, and Punjabi poetry, Dharwadker won the national translation prize given by the Sahitya Akademi, New Delhi, for *Kabir: The Weaver's Songs* (Penguin Classics, 2003, 2005). He is currently a professor of Indian languages and literatures at the University of Wisconsin, Madison.

> *I moved to the U.S. in 1981. I'm still an Indian, connected to Delhi, Jaipur, Mumbai, Pune, Chicago, and Madison.*

A Draft of Excavations

I.

For the morning
only this
      the broad chest of the fort
bared in the sun
its shoulders
        squared in stone

II.

The dead
composed this city
        stone by stone
designed their dreams
in blocks
    and slabs

made metaphors
                of mass and line
in marble granite sandstone
left us
                a labyrinth
of plinths and lintels
falling like rocks
                through time
their time our time
are stone
                stone walls stone houses
contain the wind and sand
maintain
                conspiracies of stone
by now the trees
                have skins of flint
their leaves are flakes of quartz
the wind
                is nothing but the breath
of falling arches pillars
domes
                no hand
can move aside
                these stones
III.
At dusk
                the troubled light
reveals again
the double dream
                        of mosque and fort
below the minarets
and bastions
                below the stench of slums
a blueprint history
survives
                buried under
rubble and stone

Thirty Years Ago, in a Suburb of Bombay,

Marbles behind the house with the boy next door,
who had a stump for a right arm, cut off
just below the elbow and sewn up at the end
with a nipple, budding like a boneless thumb,

who leaned forward, barefoot in the dust,
and squinted when he took aim, two white marbles
clutched for luck in the fleshy crook of his stump,
as he knocked out all of mine one by one,

changing the rules while we played that summer,
brushing aside my protests, staring me in the eye
with an older boy's contempt, daring me to leave
every time I refused to go on, until I gave in,

able always to overcome his disability
with cunning, as though he were getting back
for whatever he'd lost, all the other games
he watched me play with the boys in the neighborhood

who wouldn't play with him (bows and arrows,
catapults, French cricket), while I lay awake
at night, uneasy in the dark, still thinking
of the jarful of small bright possessions I hadn't

told my mother I'd lost in someone else's game.

ARYANIL MUKHERJEE

Aryanil Mukherjee grew up in Kolkata, India, and has published eight books of poetry and poetics, including *Kabitaar dnyakonakhaane / Another Place for* Poetry (Patralckha, 2010), *chaturangik/SQUARES* (cowritten with Pat Clifford, CinnamonTeal Press, 2009), *Sunaamir Ek Bachhar Par/One Year After The Tsunami* (Kaurab, 2008), *late night correspondence* (CinnamonTeal Press, 2008), *Hawamorager Man/Weathercock Mind* (Kaurab, 2004), and *Khelaar Naam Sabujayan/Greening Game* (Kaurab, 2000). His English poems and Spanish translations have appeared in *Big Bridge, CRIT, Drunken Boat, El Invisible Anillo* (Spain), *Helix, Jacket,* the *Literary Review, Moria, Open Spaces,* and *Rain Taxi.* An English-Bangla bidirectional translator, Mukherjee was awarded the Subhas Mukhopadhyay Memorial Award (Poetry Fortnightly Honor) in 2007. He edits the Bangla literary magazine *KAURAB*, and his own poetry has been translated into Hindi, Spanish, French, and Danish. An engineering mathematician, Mukherjee lives in Cincinnati, Ohio.

Resisting the largely monoglotic nature of American poetry, I continue to work in two languages, in between and around.

after promise

Probably nothing follows promise
White flowers of crab-apple in the left hand of spring
some spill, lay below
to grant us the much needed scent
that makes us eat well, ask well,
mend our minds so we look up to the cracker flames
hanging above the city's skull
lanterns rekindling the violets

These plateaus didn't occur like a soulful country
On the contrary, we borrowed from them

light breeze
fields, forests and figs that abscond from time to time
Lincoln park—too crowded this afternoon
The leaves are dead, instead flags of a million countries flutter

treeforms :: the touch of language

i didn't touch the language. it would have scorched my hands. the sweet sap
of bamboo shoots would have hardened to stone. the birdmeat inside would
grill all night. an immaculate lukewarm pitcher comes out of the hearth in
the morning. orangish. fitting the curves of your waist. you'd be cajoled.

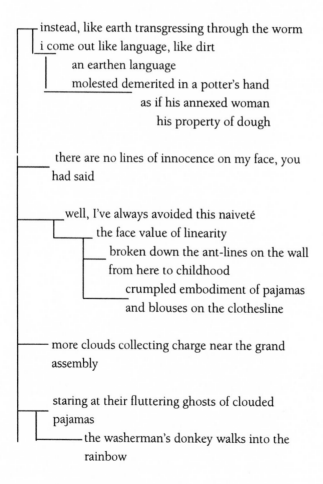

instead, like earth transgressing through the worm
i come out like language, like dirt
        an earthen language
        molested demerited in a potter's hand
                as if his annexed woman
                his property of dough

    there are no lines of innocence on my face, you
    had said

    well, I've always avoided this naiveté
        the face value of linearity
            broken down the ant-lines on the wall
            from here to childhood
                crumpled embodiment of pajamas
                and blouses on the clothesline

more clouds collecting charge near the grand
assembly

staring at their fluttering ghosts of clouded
pajamas
            the washerman's donkey walks into the
        rainbow

memory writings :: picnic

reminiscing that trip to murmur core
with *Kakali*, *Kalatan* and the evanescent green
with uncle *Banaj* careening to one corner of the frame
as the only real forester in the gang
showing us how to race along the lake with
competing images of ourselves   snarling the water
reflection remembered as transience

the fall   of leaves   defines more of a continuum
unlike the deathwish of a snapped kite to stay afloat
until an end no one sees
theater empties before the drooling titles

the rest of the party carried that spirit
gathering wood & smoke for the grill
what to fry on the side -
potatoes or eggplants?
pigeon-egg omelet or fried gramballs?
when to add bay-leaves to the frothing *Khichuri*?
a continuum   of all that euphoric trivia

felled our shadows on the picnic grounds
but not those of the lankies
did we notice?
their gradual prowl   branches lush with hunger
their green bile solidifying all around and over us
their green gush of carnivorous breath

at least two of them came down on *Sharmi*
her face, head and ribs cackled in one great rupture
wok upturned on the grill   a picnic reversed
forest feasting on human limbs

that was the inkling
left on us by the reticent forester   uncle *Banaj*
dreaded we
follow him coil to one margin of that frame

INDRAN AMIRTHANAYAGAM

Indran Amirthanayagam won the Paterson Prize in the United States for his first collection, *The Elephants of Reckoning* (Hanging Loose Press, 1993), as well as the Juegos Florales of Guayamas, Sonora, in 2006 for one of his poems in Spanish. His poetry collections include *Ceylon R.I.P.* (International Centre for Ethnic Studies, 2001), *El Infierno de los Pajaros* (Resistencia, Mexico, 2001), *El Hombre Que Recoge Nidos* (Resistencia/Conarte, Mexico, 2005) and *The Splintered Face: Tsunami Poems* (Hanging Loose Press, 2008). His awards include the New York Foundation for the Arts fellowship in poetry and a U.S.-Mexico Fund for Culture grant for his translations of the Mexican poet Manuel Ulacia. At the age of eight, he moved from Sri Lanka to London, and at fourteen he moved to Hawaii. He currently works as a U.S. diplomat. He writes poetry in English, Spanish, and French.

I am a Tamil American.

Runner

A long distance runner
paces his race,
does not exhaust himself
in a frantic flash
at the start, just to say

that once he led
the Olympic Marathon
for five miles
or even five yards.
At Munich in '72

I remember rooting
for the Sri Lankan
who sped past

the pack early on.
I wonder what's become

of that island hero
now that all the heroes
have come back
to pick up the fallen
stones, to unsalt the wells.

Has he spent his energy
on the first set of flotsam?
Perhaps he's an accountant
or clerk, some cog in an office,
and the waves have allowed

him to shine, to walk
his hands down to the beach,
to clean up the bric-a-brac
of what was once his home,
find an old snapshot among

the fallen planks: a young
man beaming framed
by two frauleins holding
tankards of frothy ale:
Munich the night before the race.

Girl Dressed

I will not forget
the girl in her Sunday dress
playing on the beach

two weeks now
after the waves razed
her house and neighborhood

but spared her and the dress
and countless other children
who will pick up seashells,

make kites from palm fronds,
hit cricket balls,
get back then to their games

and fabled innocence,
even though before the waves
civil war finished off

innocence early, sent
generations abroad
to new playing fields,

to adjust themselves
to the pleasure
and bitterness

of a nostalgia
that recalls waves
rising and breaking

shifting sands
by fisher huts, thatched
with fronds, a useless,

sweet nostalgia
for the world
before the flood

where a girl played
on the beach,
who plays still

and the flood's
a metaphor in a book
of ethics and faith—

now this modern
deluge will be
chronicled

for a girl who'll
grow tall and study,
go abroad

and recall waves,
distant and foreboding,
and her dress on a Sunday.

The City, with Elephants

The elephants of reckoning
are bunches of scruff
men and women picking up
thrown out antennae
from the rubbish
bins of the city

to fix on their tubular
bells and horn about
by oil can fires
in the freezing midnight
of the old new year.

We ride by their music
every hour in cabs on trains
hearing the pit pat
of our grown-wise pulse
shut in shut out

from the animals
of the dry season
the losers and boozers,
we must not admit our eyes
into the courtyard

the whimsy of chance
and our other excuses—
dollars in pocket—
to write beautiful songs
is all I ask, God

to do right with friends
and love a woman
and live to eighty
have people listen
to the story of my trip to America.

The elephants of reckoning
are beaten and hungry
and walk their solitary horrors
out every sunrise slurping
coffee bought with change

while in some houses
freedom-bound lovers
embrace late and read Tagore
about the people working
underneath the falling of empires.

SWATI RANA

Born in India, Swati Rana immigrated to Canada at the age of ten, before moving to the United States and attending Dartmouth College. Rana's poems have appeared in the *Berkeley Poetry Review, Salt, Main Street, Word,* and *Uncommon Threads,* and she is a recipient of the Academy of American Poets Prize and the Sidney Cox Memorial Prize. She is currently working on her first collection of poems, covering workaday life and subsistence, as well as a series of short stories about the migrations of her extended family across several continents. Rana lives in Berkeley, where she is a graduate student in the English Department at the University of California, completing a dissertation on early twentieth-century immigrant literature.

> *I am part Hyderabadi, Punjabi, and Haryanvi and take to the forests of Vermont and the Northern California coast.*

Stopping for the Northern Lights

Remnant light,
struggling against
high-walled sky

to slip around
and join the twilight
retreat. I-90's

screaming past,
but I've stopped
to watch the silent

mouthing green,
its horizoned haunt.
At my back

night rises
on each mountain, spills
to lesser hills

in shades of gray,
summons a final
farmland sweep,

congregating in a black
barn behind me.
A girl could hang

herself from such a night
—the thought folds
into my sleep

and she appears,
as sunrise
swinging from rafters.

Her interior life
is far or near
as I imagine.

But her deadpan
eyes are always open,
green and nightly.

To Reveal

I lay where the sun wasn't
in the mouth of your deep room
as you examined, with inconstant
hands, your first patient. I wore
white bloomers then,

my hair always in pigtails
curled tightly, dissonant
with this moment of undoing.
My breath evolved
to the drone of the ceiling fan,
to the slap of lizards
dropping, scurrying to dark
spaces, while you listened
with my Fisher Price stethoscope
bold and yellow like
the steady finger of light
that moved across the floor
reaching and uncovering . . .

Show me yours
and I'll show you mine,
but I, too nervous even
to look, saw only where
my mother had sewn my name
to my white bloomers,
blooming in red—
saying all the guilt
she gave me.

SUBHASHINI KALIGOTLA

Born in India, Subhashini Kaligotla was raised in the Middle East and the United States. Her poems have appeared in *Catamaran,* the *Crab Orchard Review,* the *Literary Review,* the *New England Review,* and the *Western Humanities Review* and have been anthologized in *60 Indian Poets* (Penguin India, 2008) and *The Bloodaxe Book of Contemporary Indian Poets* (Bloodaxe Books, 2008). She is a former poetry editor of *Columbia: A Journal of Literature and Art* and the current poetry editor of *Catamaran: South Asian American Writing.* Kaligotla is a graduate of Columbia University's MFA program in poetry and was awarded a Fulbright fellowship to India in 2006 for literary translation. She lives in New York City, where she is a Ph.D. candidate in art history at Columbia University.

New York City allows the happy coexistence of the many cultures and languages I inhabit and call "home."

Lepidoptera

(after El Greco's *The Crucifixion with Two Donors*)

You can't stop trawling his belly
for the navel pooled there like a fish;
the eye now follows the fallow cloth
yoking the hips to the swell

of calf on the lifted and twisted leg—
twisted (you remember) in pain;
the mind considers *mounted,* recalls
the display of Blue Morpho in a shop

on Valencia Street, the one you first
walked away from, where row after row

of glass cases lined the walls, a phalanx
of moths; but then you stepped in

(had anybody noticed?) as if to stroke
one arrested head and another, staining
your fingers lapis to compliment
the dead, fooled by mere simulacra:

straining thigh muscles, pinned arms
reaching skyward, and the body
already rigid from the ache.

Letter to New York

Walk slowly, I tell myself. *Stroll.* Being a flâneur is impossible here:
everything hurries, even the season, spilling itself like pomegranate seeds on
the pavements. So I start hurrying too, though heading nowhere.

The thin old man stands morning, evening, in vest and long sleeves left of
the subway entrance, extending a flier when I reach the top of the hill. I
used to say *No, thanks;* now I swerve away without meeting his eyes. In the
trains, the eyes are hypermyopic, unfocused—listing on the gum-streaked
floor or the windows as if looking at some television screen running the same
dull program.

Why are the underground rats more curious than your citizenry? They jerk
their heads up, left and right, as if looking for something—

A few weeks ago he said: *I can't move there.* Why should I blame him when
I'm sick of you and myself. When I've become a small person unable to
navigate a shopping cart through the Fairway aisles clogged with old people
and housewives. In the clamor of cash registers slamming under over-bright
lights and the confusion of contracting myself into smaller and smaller
packets to let variegated men through, I forget.

Why am I here? Outside I almost fall into an open cellar and wait an hour for the train and bus to take me home.

Home. Calm. After the exhausting flatulence of the caterpillar buses and the Dramamine retches of the subway train. From my double-paned windows your cabs are chrysanthemums again floating on the macadam. I am a fool to want you.

My Heart Belongs to Daddy

                When Râvan
drove down from Lanka, I climbed in

tossing my chokers along the way,
the baubles, bracelets, and bangles,

so that casuarinas assumed the aspect
and glamour of Christmas trees.

What I want?
                To stay on this island, coddled

by recalcitrant seas and jungles
prowled by red-eyed langoors.

                I'm his woman now.

MONA ALI

Mona Ali's poems have appeared in publications such as the *Asian Pacific American Journal,* and she has been invited to read at various venues, including the Joseph Papp Public Theater in New York and the Asian American Writers' Workshop. Her awards include fellowships from the Ford Foundation, the University of Cambridge, and Vassar College. Ali is an economist by profession and is currently an assistant professor at SUNY, New Paltz. She lives with her family in the Hudson Valley in New York.

I was born in Karachi, Pakistan, and hold passports of two countries, neither of which I particularly consider "home."

Noor

In the back of an anthology
a poet describes herself simply
as the mother of a newborn girl
whose name in the Arabic means sunlight, "Noor."

The reader thinks, as her own marriage falls apart,
as a new year invites her into fresh starts of grief
of her aunt, Noor, who fell in love with her cousin
Nayyar, which means moonlight,
and married him against the family's wishes.

And the reader imagines love as the boat
that must have bobbed through
clouds of ash and smoke
into the sunlight

with a crescent shaped moon for a sail.

The Wolf's Cry

A Zuihitsu

Sixteen emails in 12 hours.

•

I ask: is desire confined to language?
He writes: desire is of language and language, of earth.

•

Language?
the slippery lingual
Earth?
the slick labial
Desire?
for pulse, clavicle, even sinew

•

Letters slipping into mailboxes sublingually.

•

Does thin air carry smell quicker than heat?
I inhale the cinnamon in the bread the neighbor's baking.

•

In the back of the brain, an aching
for mint and mulberry in the tobacco
we smoked from *nargilas.*

And Fairuz rising in arabesques
from ancient amplifiers.

•

He writes: if he wore rings, would I kiss them, finger by finger?

•

How else and what to trust
except for the dreamt response.

•

Tomorrow, to sweep the silk fleece of snow
before it freezes into sleeves of ice.

•

Icicle, tricycle, circle, triangle

•

Mother calls, voice stern.
Khala has a malignant tumor.

She doesn't say breast cancer.

•

Tonight, to sleep alone
and sleeplessness.

•

He's in Rome with his new girlfriend.
He's just told me about her.

•

Loss: earth falling in on itself.

•

I write back: before you do anything foolish,
take this married woman's advice.

•

In Makmalbaf's film, Gabbeh runs away
with the horseman who serenades her,

voice disguised—only she knows—
as a wolf's cry.

•

Earth, then, also as magic carpet:
Gabbeh in the Farsi.

•

Literal translation gabbeh: rug
Plural in Urdu: *rugoon*
As in: *meri rugoon mein tayra hee khoon daurhta hai*

Trans.: Be these my veins, it is your blood that weaves through them.

•

Gabbeh runs away on the horse her lover's brought.
She rides faster, stronger than he does.

Her father chases them, fires twice.
Then returns to the tribe saying he has killed them both.

•

School children cry *zindagi rang hai:*
Life is color.
Gabbeh calls back *ishq rang hai:*
Love is color.

and wind wooing the secret ears of corn.

•

Gabbeh later reveals that Father pretended murder
so that her sisters wouldn't heed the cry of wolves.

•

No one hears canaries by the springs anymore.

•

I use The Lover's Discourse as self-help guide or manual.

•

FUTURE FACTORY:
The inscription on a card from a London gallery
I haven't decided whether to send or not send you.

•

Mahmood, tell me about Gabbeh
Does she return to her mother?

If not, do her gullible sisters
Sometimes envy death?

•

In Germany, because of racism
Your parents renamed you Christian.

Hussein in Cote d'Ivoire, Christian in Munich.

•

Love, your skin—
a river under moonlight.

It isn't hers even if it isn't mine.

•

How you courted me in German, French, English.
How you cursed me in Arabic.

•

He writes that he wants to talk,
that he's thinking of converting,

And I know, it isn't to me.

AGHA SHAHID ALI

Born in New Delhi in 1949 and raised in Kashmir, Agha Shahid Ali moved to the United States in the 1980s. His nine volumes of poetry include *Call Me Ishmael Tonight: A Book of Ghazals* (2003), *Rooms Are Never Finished* (2001), *The Country without a Post Office* (1997), and *A Nostalgist's Map of America* (1991), all published by W. W. Norton, as well as *The Beloved Witness: Selected Poems* (Viking, 1992), *A Walk through the Yellow Pages* (Sun, 1987), *The Half-Inch Himalayas* (Wesleyan University Press, 1987), *In Memory of Begum Akhtar and Other Poems* (Writers Workshop, 1979), and *Bone Sculpture* (Writers Workshop, 1972). Ali's awards included fellowships from the New York Foundation for the Arts and the Guggenheim Foundation, as well as a Pushcart Prize. He spent the last ten years of his life teaching at the University of Massachusetts, Amherst. He died on December 8, 2001.

A Pastoral

For Suvir Kaul

> on the wall the dense ivy of executions
> —ZBIGNIEW HERBERT

We shall meet again, in Srinagar,
by the gates of the Villa of Peace,
our hands blossoming into fists
till the soldiers return the keys
and disappear. Again we'll enter
our last world, the first that vanished

in our absence from the broken city.
We'll tear our shirts for tourniquets
and bind the open thorns, warm the ivy
into roses. Quick, by the pomegranate—
the bird will say—Humankind can bear
everything. No need to stop the ear

to stories rumored in branches: We'll hear
our gardener's voice, the way we did
as children, clear under trees he'd planted:
"It's true, my death, at the mosque entrance,
in the massacre, when the Call to Prayer
opened the floodgates"—Quick, follow the silence—

"and dawn rushed into everyone's eyes."
Will we follow the horned lark, pry
open the back gate into the poplar groves,
go past the search post into the cemetery,
the dust still uneasy on hurried graves
with no names, like all new ones in the city?

"It's true" (we'll hear our gardener
again). "That bird is silent all winter.
Its voice returns in spring, a plaintive cry.
That's when it saw the mountain falcon
rip open, in mid-air, the blue magpie,
then carry it, limp from the talons."

Pluck the blood: My words will echo thus
at sunset, by the ivy, but to what purpose?
In the drawer of the cedar stand,
white in the verandah, we'll find letters:
When the post offices died, the mailman
knew we'd return to answer them. Better

if he let them speed to death,
blacked out by Autumn's Press Trust—
not like this, taking away our breath,
holding it with love's anonymous
scripts: "See how your world has cracked.
Why aren't you here? Where are you? Come back.

Is history deaf there, across the oceans?"
Quick, the bird will say. And we'll try

the keys, with the first one open the door
into the drawing room. Mirror after mirror,
textiled by dust, will blind us to our return
as we light oil lamps. The glass map of our country,

still on the wall, will tear us to lace—
We'll go past our ancestors, up the staircase,
holding their wills against our hearts. Their wish
was we return—forever!—and inherit (Quick, the bird
will say) that to which we belong, not like this—
to get news of our death after the world's.

Ghazal

The only language of loss left in the world is Arabic—
These words were said to me in a language not Arabic.

Ancestors, you've left me a plot in the family graveyard—
Why must I look, in your eyes, for prayers in Arabic?

Majnoon, his clothes ripped, still weeps for Laila.
O, this is the madness of the desert, his crazy Arabic.

Who listens to Ishmael? Even now he cries out:
Abraham, throw away your knives, recite a psalm in Arabic.

From exile Mahmoud Darwish writes to the world:
You'll all pass between the fleeting words of Arabic.

The sky is stunned, it's become a ceiling of stone.
I tell you it must weep. So kneel, pray for rain in Arabic.

At an exhibition of miniatures, such delicate calligraphy:
Kashmiri paisleys tied into the golden hair of Arabic!

The Koran prophesied a fire of men and stones.
Well, it's all now come true, as it was said in the Arabic.

When Lorca died, they left the balconies open and saw:
his *qasidas* braided, on the horizon, into knots of Arabic.

Memory is no longer confused, it has a homeland—
Says Shammas: Territorialize each confusion in a graceful
    Arabic.

Where there were homes in Deir Yassein, you'll see dense
    forests—
That village was razed. There's no sign of Arabic.

I too, O Amichai, saw the dresses of beautiful women.
And everything else, just like you, in Death, Hebrew, and
    Arabic.

They ask me to tell them what *Shahid* means—
Listen: It means "The Belovéd" in Persian, "witness" in Arabic.

Footnote to History

    For Bari Károly

    Gypsies . . . coming originally from India to Europe a thousand
    years ago . . .

On the banks of the Indus,
just before

    it reaches
    the ocean,

and just before
the monsoons,

                    they left
                    me clutching

islands of farewells.

For ten centuries
they sent no word

though I often heard
through seashells

ships whispering for help.

I stuffed my pockets
with the sounds of wrecks.

I still can't decipher
scripts of storms

as I leaf through
the river's waves.

Half-torn by the wind,
their words reach

the shore, demanding
I memorize their

                    ancient and recent
                    journeys in

caravans ambushed by
forests on fire.

At the Museum

But in 2500 B.C. Harappa,
who cast in bronze a servant girl?

No one keeps records
of soldiers and slaves.

The sculptor knew this,
polishing the ache

off her fingers stiff
from washing the walls

and scrubbing the floors,
from stirring the meat

and the crushed asafoetida
in the bitter gourd.

But I'm grateful she smiled
at the sculptor,

as she smiles at me
in bronze,

a child who had to play woman
to her lord

when the warm June rains
came to Harappa.

PIREENI SUNDARALINGAM

Pireeni Sundaralingam's poetry has appeared in journals such as *Plough-shares, World Literature Today,* and *Cyphers* (Éire), as well as *the Guardian* newspaper (UK) and anthologies such as *Three Genres* (Prentice-Hall, 2009), *Language for a New Century: Poetry from the Middle East, Asia and Beyond* (W. W. Norton, 2008), and *Masala* (Macmillan, 2005). Her poetry has been broadcast on NPR, BBC, and Swedish National Radio, and been translated into French, Italian, Swedish, and Gaelic. Educated at the University of Oxford, Sundaralingam has held scientific research posts at MIT and UCLA. She was awarded national fellowships in both cognitive science and poetry and has given papers on the intersections between poetry and neuroscience at the Museum of Modern Art (New York), the Exploratorium (San Francisco), and the Life in Space symposium at Studio Olafur Eliasson (Berlin). Born in Sri Lanka and raised both there and in England, she currently lives in San Francisco.

Having witnessed ethnic violence in two countries, I find common ground with all those who work toward social unity.

Lot's Wives

We stood,
as women before us have stood,

looking back at our burning cities,
watching the smoke
rise from our empty homes.

It was quiet then. And cold.

We heard their cries, the caged birds
clawing at their perches, our daughters
naked in the hungry mob.

Such death. The smell of justice
drifting on the burnt wind.

We saw it all,
saw the fire fall like rain,

saw our tears
track stiff, white veins
down our bodies,

saw the brine crawl
through salt-cracked skin.

Now, turning in the restless night,
we dream we stand there still,
alone on the hill's black belly.

We, the forgotten,
whose names were swallowed by God.

Vermont, 1885

Each year we disappear
into the formless white, the snow erasing
mile upon mile of our neighbors' farms.
Preacher says, so shall we all
come unto Judgment Day, diminished
by the level gaze of God.

I go home to my attic's silence, adjust
focal length and lenses, grind out
the sea-green glass. Microscope
and camera: beneath their quiet stare
the snow disappears, is replaced
by a single, unique, six-pointed star.

*Aged 19, W.A. Bentley was the first to photograph a snowflake, later formulating the
theory that no two snowflakes have the same structure.*

Language Like Birds

It is Paris, Berlin, New York,
    it is any one of countless cities, any one
        of endless lands in which we find ourselves,

our careless hurrying through crowds
    cut short, silenced in one moment

by the sight of teeth and hands and jaw,
    by the familiarity of bone.

These are the faces that reflect our own,
    the eyes of exiles that will search

and search again for patterns in the skin,
    kinship in the bones,
        history in the hand-shape of strangers.

But we have no words to express our loss, no tools
    to measure out the length of our leaving.

Fleeing before the war's black howl,
    we left behind language
        words too heavy a burden to carry.

Destiny.   Family.   Fate.

These are the words that remain
    when we find each other in foreign lands,

when we break open each word of our language
    to share, to savor, to set free.

We open our throats and language,
    like birds, bursts from our lips, words

exploding across city streets, brief
    as the violence of gunfire.

JEET THAYIL

Jeet Thayil was born in Kerala, India, and educated in Hong Kong, New York, and Bombay. His four poetry collections include *These Errors Are Correct* (Tranquebar Books, 2008) and *English* (Penguin/Rattapallax, 2004), and he is the editor of *The Bloodaxe Book of Contemporary Indian Poets* (Bloodaxe, 2008) and *Divided Time: India and the End of Diaspora* (Routledge, 2006). His writing has appeared in *London Magazine, Verse, Stand, Agenda, Poets and Writers,* the *Cortland Review, Drunken Boat,* the *Independent,* and the *Poetry Review.* He is a contributing editor to *Fulcrum,* a Boston-based poetry annual, and an editor of the multimedia arts journal *Rattapallax.* Thayil is a recipient of grants and awards from the New York Foundation for the Arts, the Rockefeller Foundation, the British Council, and the Swiss Arts Council. In 2004, he moved from New York to New Delhi and currently lives in Bombay.

> *I am a Malayali Hongkonger, Bombayman, and New Yorker (not*
> *American), and my nation is the Republic of English.*

September 10, 2001

How much harder it is to speak
when I have spent the whole day silent.
I would like to stop someone,
leave my room in the evening
and stop someone, a man without hope,
or a woman bent double, as if she were
searching the sidewalk for gems
caught in the cracks, and I would tell her
that each of us walks with the same
impossible burden, knowing
that only the stars will last—
she will listen to me, hear what I say
and go on her way, bent over as before,
never looking up at the approaching sky.

from *Premonition*

1.

To see if I'd still be here,
looking back at you, my figure
still, yours in motion, our
minds receding into the future,
the miles between us stretched like wire.
In my dream, it was a Sunday in summer
when you returned to the East River.
The city's last dogwood shivered
in the sun, but you didn't see her.
On the subway (your token had expired
years ago), you said, *Nothing's sadder
than this.* We found seats together.
I reached for you, but you weren't there.
Someone looked at me with pity and fear.

with a first line by Theresa Burns

2.

When it rains, the dead descend, you appear,
the smell of rainwater in your hair,

wearing the ring I placed on your finger,
a scent like heat and a voice not yours, a
child's voice singing of age-old danger,
in Hindi, a lover's lament from *Pyaasa*.

Your lips, clear of the color you wear,
are not new to me, are lovely and bare,

and our old argument still burns.
How soon will you forget me if I die?
By the river in this room and the way it returns,
I swear, If I forget you, let everything die.

When it rains the dead ascend, disappear
where we cannot follow, into the living air.

with a first line by Michelle Yasmin Valladares

Letter from a Mughal Emperor, 2006

Nothing here's worth a tick.

I hid everything except the heads. They respect slaughter.

They respect only slaughter. They forget the other things we brought them, the ghazals, the gardens, the ice and symmetry.

It's an affliction to grow up motherless, with your lady mother living beside you.

They have many images, but they have no God. They're fit only for war.

Even the dogs are second rate.

In Tashkent I had no money, no country or hope of one, only humiliation. But among the people I found much beauty. No pears are better.

There are no accidents. There's only God.

Tending to his doves on the eve of battle, my father flew into a ravine at the fortress of Akhsi.

He became a falcon. I became emperor.

Sometimes, when I eat a Kabul melon, I remember my father and you.

I've forgotten more than I've seen, but I haven't forgotten enough.

There's only one way to live in a place like this, with your disgust close at hand.

One night I took majoun because the moon was shining. The next day I took some more, at sunrise.

I enjoyed wonderful fields of flowers, flowers on all sides. I saw an apple sapling with five or six leaves placed regularly on each branch.

No painter could have done this.

I made a schedule. Saturday, Sunday, Tuesday and Wednesday for wine, the other days for majoun.

Your letter puzzled me:

The people are caught between constant spiritual anguish and a faith that will give meaning to the question that consumes them: the dual substance of Krishna, the yearning of man to know God. Between the spirit and the flesh, a great unwinnable war.

Dear friend, write clearly, with plain words. Writing badly will make you ill.

Once, in an orchard, I was sick with fever and vision. I was young, but I prepared myself.

A hundred years or a day, in the end you'll leave this place.

Long ago, my grandfather's face looked into mine, I think with love.

Now we speak of ghazals, of metrics and rhyme or our most famous massacres.

When he conquered Lahore he planted a banana tree. It thrived, even in that climate.

His memory is so good it gives him a second life. Mine gives only a partial one.

It's no more than I need.

Flight

How did we know to go, to obey?
How did we come to be refugees,

our household scattered, an eastward breeze
our guide? We were ghosts, not from the past

but from a future that would last
no longer than a season.

We hoped to be led by a star or by reason,
but were taken by circumstance, by its

furious, arbitrary dance, like poets
of a line defined by rhyme,

our stanzas shaped by chance and time.
The slanted lines and inverted minarets

of Arabic, on successive jets,
took us 8,000 miles from the city,

from the impossibility
of our lives. We were headed

home, but home wasn't where we'd left it.
Here, nothing moves but wilts. The banyan

digs its fingers in for rain,
and finds the sun. Bird cries fill the sky.

Of them all, the koel it is whose song I
hear all night long, a coagulating widow's

song that clogs the windows
and the ears. Like the unreliable,

the inconsolable koel
who makes her home where she finds it,

I make my home with you, in transit.
The continent drops away and reappears,

its slow, ash-choked rivers rehearse
a brilliant future from a time long gone,

and the koel rehearses her song,
You and you are here to stay.

Acknowledgments

HOMRAJ ACHARYA, "The Silk-Cotton Tree." Copyright © 2001 by Homraj Acharya. Originally appeared in *Salt Hill Journal*. Reprinted by permission of the author. "The Kerosene Stove." Copyright © 2001 by Homraj Acharya. Originally appeared in *Strategic Confusion*. Reprinted by permission of the author.

DILRUBA AHMED, "Invitation." Copyright © 2005 by Dilruba Ahmed. Originally appeared in *Crab Orchard Review*. Reprinted by permission of the author. "The 18th Century Weavers of Muslin Whose Thumbs Were Chopped." Copyright © 2010 by Dilruba Ahmed. Originally appeared in *Many Mountains Moving*. Reprinted by permission of the author. "Learning." Copyright © by Dilruba Ahmed. Reprinted by permission of the author.

MEENA ALEXANDER, "River and Bridge" from *River and Bridge*. Copyright © 1995 by Meena Alexander. Reprinted with permission from Toronto South Asian Review Publications. "September Sunlight" and "Color of Home" from the poem cycle "Letters to Lorca," and "Slow Dancing" from the poem cycle "Letters to Gandhi" from *Raw Silk*. Copyright © 2004 by Meena Alexander. Reprinted by permission of Northwestern University Press.

AGHA SHAHID ALI, "A Pastoral," "Ghazal," "At the Museum," and "Footnote to History" from *The Country Without a Post Office*. Copyright © 1997 by Agha Shahid Ali. Reprinted by permission of W. W. Norton & Company, Inc.

KAZIM ALI, "The River's Address," "Event," and "Thicket" from *The Far Mosque*. Copyright © 2005 by Kazim Ali. Reprinted by permission of Alice James Books.

MONA ALI, "The Wolf's Cry." Copyright © 2002 by Mona Ali. Originally appeared in *The Asian Pacific American Journal*. Reprinted by permission of the author. "Noor." Copyright © 2003 by Mona Ali. Originally appeared in *Dial Magazine*. Reprinted by permission of the author.

INDRAN AMIRTHANAYAGAM, "The City, with Elephants" from *The Elephants of Reckoning* (Hanging Loose Press). Copyright © 1993 by Indran Amirthanayagam. Reprinted by permission of the author. "Runner" and "Girl Dressed" from *The Splintered Face: Tsunami Poems* (Hanging Loose Press). Copyright © 2008 by Indran Amirthanayagam. Reprinted by permission of the author.

NEELANJANA BANERJEE, "Priapos" and "Cowgirl Series I." Copyright © by Neelanjana Banerjee. Reprinted by permission of the author.

RAVI CHANDRA, "Cleanup on Aisle #3" and "The Old Man Speaks." Copyright © by Ravi Chandra. Reprinted by permission of the author.

VINAY DHARWADKER, "Thirty Years Ago, in a Suburb of Bombay" and "A Draft of Excavations" from *Sunday at the Lodi Gardens* (Viking). Copyright ©1994 by Vinay Dharwadker. Reprinted by permission of the author.

CHITRA BANERJEE DIVAKARUNI, "Yuba City School" and "Two Women Outside a Circus, Pushkar" from *Black Candle*. Copyright © 1991 by Chitra Banerjee Divakaruni. Reprinted by permission of CALYX Books. "The Geography Lesson" and "Indian Movie, New Jersey" from *Leaving Yuba City* (Doubleday). Copyright © 1998 by Chitra Banerjee Divakaruni. Reprinted by permission of the author.

MONICA FERRELL, "In the Binary Alleys of the Lion's Virus" from *Beasts for the Chase* (Sarabande Books). Copyright © 2008 by Monica Ferrell. Reprinted by permission of the author. "Love, the Kunstkammer Version." Copyright © 2009 by Monica Ferrell. Originally appeared in *The Literary Review*. Reprinted by permission of the author. "The Coin of Your Country" and "Confessions of Beatrice D'Este." Copyright © by Monica Ferrell. Reprinted by permission of the author.

RO GUNETILLEKE, "Lost Column." Copyright © 2006 by Ro Gunetilleke. Originally appeared in *Poetic Diversity*. Reprinted by permission of the author. "Spirited Away." Copyright © 2009 by Ro Gunetilleke. Originally appeared in *Muse India*. Reprinted by permission of the author.

MOHAMMAD FAISAL HADI, "My Uncle, Failing to Slaughter the Goat of His 12th Eid," "Fatima," and "Public Benefits." Copyright © by Mohammad Faisal Hadi. Reprinted by permission of author.

MINAL HAJRATWALA, "Angerfish," "Miss Indo-America dreams," and "Generica/America." Copyright © by Minal Hajratwala. Reprinted by permission of author.

MYTILI JAGANNATHAN, "nationalism redactor." Copyright © 1999 by Mytili Jagannathan. Originally appeared in *Combo*. Reprinted by permission of the author. "Dream House." Copyright © 2000 by Mytili Jagannathan. Originally appeared in *Interlope*. Reprinted by permission of the author.

VIVEK JAIN, "Anand's Story," "Poem for a Would Be Revolutionary, My Father," and December, 1984." Copyright © by Vivek Jain. Reprinted by permission of the author.

SUMMI KAIPA, "Excerpts from *The Epics*" from *The Epics* (Leroy Press). Copyright © 1999 by Summi Kaipa. Reprinted by permission of the author. "Excerpts from *A Personal Cinema*." Copyright © by Summi Kaipa. Originally appeared in *The Literary Review.* Reprinted by permission of the author.

SUBHASHINI KALIGOTLA, "Lepidoptera." Copyright © 2007 by Subhashini Kaligotla. Originally appeared in *Crab Orchard Review.* Reprinted by permission of the author. "My Heart Belongs to Daddy" and "Letter to New York." Copyright © by Subhashini Kaligotla. Reprinted by permission of the author.

BHANU KAPIL, "Excerpt from *Humanimal [A project for future children].*" Copyright © 2009 by Bhanu Kapil. Reprinted by permission of Kelsey Street Press.

VANDANA KHANNA, "Hair," "Dot Head," "Blackwater Fever," and "Echo" from *Train to Agra* (Southern Illinois University Press). Copyright © 2001 by Vandana Khanna. Reprinted by permission of the author.

MAYA KHOSLA, "Return to Grand Canyon," "Under Wolf-Paw," and "Oppenheimer quotes *The Bhagavad Gita*" from *Keel Bone* (Bear Star Press). Copyright © 2003 by Maya Khosla. Reprinted by permission of author. "Sequoia Sempervirens." Copyright © by Maya Khosla. Reprinted by permission of author.

AMITAVA KUMAR, "Mistaken Identity" from *No Tears for the NRI* (Writers Workshop). Copyright © 1996 by Amitava Kumar. Reprinted by permission of author. "Against Nostalgia" from *Bombay-London-NewYork* (Routledge) Copyright © 2002 by Amitava Kumar. Reprinted by permission of the author.

BHARGAVI C. MANDAVA, "Moonsweets." Copyright © 1996 by Bhargavi C. Mandava. Originally appeared in *Another Way to Dance: Contemporary Asian Poetry* (TSAR Publications). Reprinted by permission of author. "Of Starry Silence." Copyright © 2001 by Bhargavi C. Mandava. Originally published in *Through a Child's Eyes: Poems and Stories about War* (Plain View Press). Reprinted by permission of author.

TANUJA MEHROTRA, "Nainital." Copyright © 1999 by Tanuja Mehrotra. Originally appeared in *The Asian Pacific American Journal*. Reprinted by permission of author. "Manthara" and "Song for New Orleans." Copyright © by Tanuja Mehrotra. Reprinted by permission of author.

VIKAS MENON, "Radha." Copyright © 2000 by Vikas Menon. Originally appeared in *Toronto Review*. Reprinted by permission of author. "Drown" and "Urdu Funk." Copyright © 2007 by Vikas Menon. Originally appeared in *MiPOesias*. Reprinted by permission of author.

FAISAL MOHYUDDIN, "Ayodhya." Copyright © 2006 by Faisal Mohyuddin. Originally appeared in *Atlanta Review*. Reprinted by permission of author. "Blood Harmonies." Copyright © 2007 by Faisal Mohyuddin. Originally appeared in *Poet Lore*. Reprinted by permission of author. "Poem Inspired by a Note Found Scrawled Onto the Inside Cover of *One Day at a Time in Al-Anon* Sitting on a Bookshelf at Café Ambrosia, Evanston, Illinois." Copyright © by Faisal Mohyuddin. Reprinted by permission of author.

ARYANIL MUKHERJEE, "treeforms :: the touch of language" and "after promise" from *Late Night Correspondence* (CinnamonTeal Press). Copyright © 2008 by Aryanil Mukherjee. Reprinted by permission of author. "memory writings :: picnic." Copyright © by Aryanil Mukherjee. Reprinted by permission of author.

REENA NARAYAN, "Tobacco Wrapped in *The Fiji Times*" and "My Daughter." Copyright © by Reena Narayan. Reprinted by permission of author.

RALPH NAZARETH, "Horse Play," "Red Eye," and "A Question for Vaclav Havel" from *Ferrying Secrets* (Yugadi Publishers). Copyright © 2005 by Ralph Nazareth. Reprinted by permission of author.

AIMEE NEZHUKUMATATHIL, "Fishbone" and "Mr. Mustard's Dance Club: Ladies' Night" from *Miracle Fruit* (Tupelo Press). Copyright © 2003 by Aimee Nezhukumatathil. Reprinted by permission of author. "Last Aerogramme to You, With Lizard" from *At the Drive-in Volcano* (Tupelo Press). Copyright © 2007 by Aimee Nezhukumatathil. Reprinted by permission of author. "The Mascot of Beavercreek High Breaks Her Silence." Copyright © by Aimee Nezhukumatathil. Reprinted by permission of author.

SASHA KAMINI PARMASAD, "The Old Man." Copyright © 2005 by Sasha Kamini Parmasad. Originally appeared in the *Jamaica Observer.* Reprinted by permission of author. "Sugarcane Farmer" and "Burning." Copyright © 2009 by Sasha Kamini Parmasad. Originally appeared in *Muse India.* Reprinted by permission of author.

R. PARTHASARATHY, "Exile 3, 4, 5, 6, and 7" from *Rough Passage* (Oxford University Press India). Copyright © 1990 by R. Parthasarathy. Reprinted by permission of author. "Remembered Village." Copyright © 2000 by R. Parthasarathy. Originally appeared in *Verse.* Reprinted by permission of author. "The Concise Kamasutra." Copyright © 2005 by R. Parthasarathy. Originally appeared in *Fulcrum.* Reprinted by permission of author.

in *The New Yorker.* Reprinted by permission of author. "Elegy" and "The Dream I Didn't Have." Copyright © 2008 by Vijay Seshadri. Originally appeared in *Epiphany.* Reprinted by permission of author.

PURVI SHAH, "Made in India, Immigrant Song #3," "Unhoming," and "Nature's Acre, POSTED" from *Terrain Tracks* (New Rivers Press). Copyright © 2006 by Purvi Shah. Reprinted by permission of author.

SEJAL SHAH, "Everybody's Greatest Hits." Copyright © 2005 by Sejal Shah. Originally appeared in *The Asian Pacific American Journal.* Reprinted by permission of author. "Accordion" and "Independence, Iowa." Copyright © by Sejal Shah. Reprinted by permission of author.

RAVI SHANKAR, "Return to Mumbai," "Before Sunrise, San Francisco," and "The Flock's Reply to the Passionate Shepherd" from *Instrumentality* (Cherry Grove). Copyright © 2004 by Ravi Shankar. Reprinted by permission of author.

PRAGEETA SHARMA, "Paper" and "Paper II" from *Bliss to Fill* (Subpress). Copyright © 2000 by Prageeta Sharma. Reprinted by permission of author. "I Cannot Forget You" and "In Open Water, in Mathematical Star." Copyright © by Prageeta Sharma. Reprinted by permission of author.

PIREENI SUNDARALINGAM, "Lot's Wives." Copyright © 2003 by Pireeni Sundaralingam. Originally appeared in *Ploughshares.* Reprinted by permission of author. "Language Like Birds." Copyright © 2008 Pireeni Sundaralingam. Originally published in *World Literature Today.* Reprinted by permission of author. "Vermont, 1885." Copyright © by Pireeni Sundaralingam. Reprinted by permission of the author.

JEET THAYIL, "September 10, 2001" from *English* (Rattapallax Press). Copyright © 2004 by Jeet Thayil. Reprinted by permission of Penguin/ Rattapallax. "From *Premonition*," "Letter from a Mughal Emperor, 2006" and "Flight" from *These Errors Are Correct* by Jeet Thayil (Tranquebar Books). Copyright © 2008 by Jeet Thayil. Reprinted by permission of Tranquebar Books.

Author Index

Title Index

NEELANJANA BANERJEE's work has appeared in *The Literary Review, Asian Pacific American Journal, Nimrod,* and the anthology *Desilicious.* In 2007 she received an MFA in Creative Writing from San Francisco State University. She has taught creative writing throughout the San Francisco Bay Area for organizations like WritersCorps and Kearny Street Workshop. Banerjee has worked in mainstream, ethnic, and independent media for the past ten years. For over five years she helped young people tell their own stories at YO! Youth Outlook Multimedia. She is an editor and blogger with the Asian American magazine *Hyphen,* where she now oversees the semiannual short story contest.

SUMMI KAIPA received an MFA in Poetry from the Iowa Writers' Workshop and is the author of three chapbooks. Kaipa was the founder and editor of *Interlope,* a magazine featuring innovative writing by Asian Americans (1998–2003) and served as a board member and literary curator for several San Francisco nonprofits, including the Alliance of Emerging Creative Artists (AECA), an organization promoting emerging Asian American artists, and New Langton Arts. She has also judged several literary awards, including the Potrero Nuevo Fund Prize. In addition to being a writer Kaipa is a clinical psychologist. She lives in Berkeley, California, with her husband.

PIREENI SUNDARALINGAM's poetry has appeared in journals such as *Ploughshares, The Progressive,* and *World Literature Today,* as well as anthologies such as *Masala* (Macmillan, 2005) and *Language for a New Century: Poetry from the Middle East, Asia and Beyond* (W.W. Norton, 2008). She has served on award juries for several literary organizations and festivals, including PEN Oakland and the Neustadt International Prize for Literature. Together with coproducer Colm Ó Riain, she commissioned and curated twenty-one poets and musicians to tell the forgotten immigration stories of America; the resulting recorded album, *Bridge Across the Blue,* was awarded the Potrero Nuevo Fund Prize.